WALK IN THE LIGHT OF THE LORD

Walk in the Light of the Lord

A Thought a Day for Advent and Christmastide

HAROLD A. BUETOW, PHD, JD

ST PAULS

Alba
House

Library of Congress Cataloging-in-Publication Data

Buetow, Harold A.
Walk in the light of the Lord : a thought a day for Advent and Christmastide / Harold A. Buetow.
p. cm.
ISBN 0-8189-0964-1
1. Advent. 2. Christmas. 3. Bible—Homiletical use. 4. Catholic Church—Liturgy. I. Title.

BX2170.A4B84 2004
251'.61—dc22
2003025576

Produced and designed in the United States of America by the Fathers and Brothers of the Society of St. Paul, 2187 Victory Boulevard, Staten Island, NY 10314-6603, as part of their communications apostolate.

ISBN: 0-8189-0964-1

Printing Information:

Current Printing - first digit	1	2	3	4	5	6	7	8	9	10

Year of Current Printing - first year shown

2004	2005	2006	2007	2008	2009	2010	2011	2012	2013

Poor that we are in giving thanks,
I would like to try to thank the goodness, kindness,
and graciouness given me in this work by
Dr. Rose M. Auteri,
Patricia C. Deeley,
Steven Krogman, and
Col. (Ret.) Michael L. Wardinski, Ph.D.

Biblical Abbreviations

OLD TESTAMENT

Genesis	Gn	Nehemiah	Ne	Baruch	Ba
Exodus	Ex	Tobit	Tb	Ezekiel	Ezk
Leviticus	Lv	Judith	Jdt	Daniel	Dn
Numbers	Nb	Esther	Est	Hosea	Ho
Deuteronomy	Dt	1 Maccabees	1 M	Joel	Jl
Joshua	Jos	2 Maccabees	2 M	Amos	Am
Judges	Jg	Job	Jb	Obadiah	Ob
Ruth	Rt	Psalms	Ps	Jonah	Jon
1 Samuel	1 S	Proverbs	Pr	Micah	Mi
2 Samuel	2 S	Ecclesiastes	Ec	Nahum	Na
1 Kings	1 K	Song of Songs	Sg	Habakkuk	Hab
2 Kings	2 K	Wisdom	Ws	Zephaniah	Zp
1 Chronicles	1 Ch	Sirach	Si	Haggai	Hg
2 Chronicles	2 Ch	Isaiah	Is	Malachi	Ml
Ezra	Ezr	Jeremiah	Jr	Zechariah	Zc
		Lamentations	Lm		

NEW TESTAMENT

Matthew	Mt	Ephesians	Eph	Hebrews	Heb
Mark	Mk	Philippians	Ph	James	Jm
Luke	Lk	Colossians	Col	1 Peter	1 P
John	Jn	1 Thessalonians	1 Th	2 Peter	2 P
Acts	Ac	2 Thessalonians	2 Th	1 John	1 Jn
Romans	Rm	1 Timothy	1 Tm	2 John	2 Jn
1 Corinthians	1 Cor	2 Timothy	2 Tm	3 John	3 Jn
2 Corinthians	2 Cor	Titus	Tt	Jude	Jude
Galatians	Gal	Philemon	Phm	Revelation	Rv

Table of Contents

Christmas Season

Introduction

FOREWORD

One dreary evening in November, a stranger rode into a small town. He stopped his horse in front of a lonely storefront. The windows were boarded shut and the door was locked. But the man looked at it, smiled, and said, "It will do."

All through the short gray days and the long dark nights of that month, the man worked. The townspeople could hear the faint pam, pam, pam of his hammer, and the snish, snish, snish of his saw. They could smell the clean scent of new lumber and the deep smell of new paint. But no one knew who the man was or what he was doing. All the townspeople just waited, and watched, and wondered.

But one small girl waited longer than she could stand. So one snowy day she knocked at the stranger's door. "Hello," she said. "My name is Lucy. Do you need some help?"

The man smiled warmly and nodded. Then he opened the door, and Lucy stepped inside.

A long counter ran down one side of the room. Bare shelves filled the opposite walls. In the back were dozens of barrels and crates.

"Can you help me unpack?" the man asked.

Lucy said, "Sure," but her heart sank at the sight of all the boxes. What if they were only barrels of nails and bags of flour? But she removed her dripping boots and hung her coat on a peg. On stocking feet, she crossed the rough wooden floor and knelt beside a crate.

"Please. Open it," the man urged.

Slowly, Lucy put her hand into the box and pulled out an object wrapped in tissue. Round and heavy, it almost slipped through her trembling fingers. It was a glass jar.

Lucy gave the man a puzzled look. "Go on," his nod said.

So she unpacked other glass jars, until she was completely surrounded by jars of all shapes and sizes: tall and thin, round and squat, jars with lids and jars without.

"Now," the man said, "for something to put inside." And he pulled over a huge crate. As Lucy unpacked it, her eyes lit up. It was candy. Her favorite: gumdrops!

"Try some," the man said.

She popped one in her mouth. Now she could hardly unwrap fast enough. Peppermint sticks! Taffy! Lollipops! Chocolates!

Wide-eyed, she looked at the man. "Welcome to Lindeman's Candy Store, Lucy. I'm John Lindeman."

Soon the small store was filled with candies, gleaming in their glass jars. And the aromas!

Then, in the very last package in the very last crate, was a candy Lucy had never seen before: a red-and-white striped candy stick with a bend on the end. "What's this?" Lucy asked.

"This," Mr. Lindeman explained, "is a candy cane. It's a very special Christmas candy."

"Why?" Lucy asked.

"Tell me," Mr. Lindeman asked in turn, "What letter does it look like?" Lucy took the candy and turned it in her hand.

"J!" she said.

"Yes," Mr. Lindeman smiled. "J for Jesus, who was born on Christmas day. Now turn it over. What does it remind you of?"

Lucy turned the candy in her hand. She peered down intently. "I know!" she said finally. "It's like a shepherd's staff."

"Who were the first to find out about Jesus' birth?" Mr. Lindeman asked.

"Shepherds in the field," Lucy answered, and then asked, "But Mr. Lindeman, what are the stripes for?"

The man's eyes grew sad. "The prophet Isaiah said, 'By his stripes we are healed.' Before he died on the cross, Jesus was stripped and beaten. He bled terribly. The red reminds us of his suffering and his blood."

"But then," Mr. Lindeman continued, "the candy is white as well. When we give our lives to Jesus, his blood washes away our sins, making us white and pure as snow. That," he said, "is the story of the candy cane. It's a story that needs to be told. Will you help me share it?"

In the depths of December, the town was whipped by blizzard winds. For days, the sun hid itself. But every morning, Mr. Lindeman and Lucy ventured out. They wore heavy woolen coats and bright hand-knit scarves. And in their stiff, mittened fingers they each held a bag.

They went to every house in town. In every home in which they told the story, they left a small gift of candy and gave an invitation.

On the afternoon of Christmas Eve, the sun finally broke through the clouds. And Lindeman's Candy Store officially opened. The mayor came, and the young wives, and the farmers. The children ran in dizzy circles. They had come to share in the opening of the candy store, but they shared something more. Something bigger. Something better. They shared the story of the candy cane.

Actually, the candy cane had been born over 350 years before, when mothers used white sugar sticks as pacifiers for their babies. Around 1670, the choirmaster of the cathedral in Cologne, Germany, bent the sticks into canes to represent a shepherd's staff. He used these white candy canes to keep the attention of small children during the long Nativity service.

In the mid-1800's, the candy cane arrived in the United States. The red stripe, and at times a green one, was added at the turn of the century, when peppermint and wintergreen became traditional flavors.

LITURGICAL YEAR

The liturgy of the Church's Advent-Christmas season commemorates what that candy cane stands for. Liturgy is a dialogue and exchange in which God comes to people in the Holy Spirit, speaks to them in His Word, and acts on them in Sacrament before people reply in prayer and sacrifice through Christ in the Holy Spirit.

Just as the Church uses *material things* to uplift and supernaturalize our earthly life, so does she use *time* to sanctify people and lead them gradually to eternity. She does that by means of her liturgical year. A feast day or season was from their beginning a special time intended to focus attention on some aspect of Jesus and the notion of his saving us all.

Before we go into the liturgical year and the Advent-Christmas part of it, it's good to remind ourselves of the breakdown of time into weeks and days. The existence of the seven-day week was implied in the creation story of the first chapter of the Book of Genesis. Whereas Judaism used a specific name only for the Sabbath (*shabbat*) and numbered the rest of the days from it, in regions of the dominant culture in the time of Christ, the Greek, the days of the week were linked with the "seven planets" (the five known at that time, plus the sun and the moon). But since the planets were dedicated to the principal gods, the days of the week were named after them, too.

Sunday, which was special for Christians, didn't arise out of the Jewish Sabbath, or Saturday: In fact, the first Christians kept both Sabbath and Sunday. Rather, Christians have from the first come together on Sunday to anticipate the second coming of the Lord, to encounter the risen Christ in the Eucharist, and to recall the Resurrection of Jesus.

Whereas the last day of the week was sacred to the Jews as the day on which creation was finished, the first day is sacred to Christians as the day of the new creation begun in the Lord's Resurrection. The early Christian Fathers also exploited the symbolism based on the Greco-Roman (originally Egyptian) name for this day, namely "day of the sun" (*dies solis*), from which the Anglo-Saxon name "Sunday" is derived.

Calling Sunday "the Lord's day" (*dies dominica,* mentioned in the New Testament only in Rv 1:10) was quickly adopted by Christians, and in time replaced the "day of the sun" as the legal name for the day. It's preserved to our time in the romance languages as *domenica, domingo*, and *dimanche*.

From the very beginning Sunday bore a joyous character. At Sunday Mass the Church becomes visible in her members gathered about the heavenly Father's table to celebrate the Eucharistic sacrificial meal. The members make present the Lord's redemptive action. The assembly gives the individual the sense of belonging — of belonging to a family of brothers and sisters whose Father is God, whose elder brother is Jesus, and whose joy is to live for each other.

Before the legal toleration of Christianity, Sunday was a workday; Christian worship was confined to the night and early morning hours. The Emperor Constantine introduced the first civil legislation concerning Sunday rest in 321 A.D., when he decreed that all work should cease on Sunday, except farming when necessary. The cessation of work on Sunday was introduced less to allow for rest than to clear the way for intense spiritual activity: Go to church, listen to the scriptures and homilies, meditate on heavenly things. Scriptural excerpts were assigned to daily worship.

Sacred Scripture "is of the greatest importance in the celebration of the liturgy" (Vatican Council II, *Constitution on the Sacred Liturgy*, 24). The most important place for the reading of scripture in all liturgies from the earliest days of the Church has been the Mass. "The liturgy of the Word and the Eucharist are so closely connected with each other that they form but one single act of worship" (*Ibid.* 56).

Through the lectors — readers — at the liturgy, God speaks a living, active word which, even if it's being heard for the thousandth time, should sound as new as when it was first proclaimed. God is speaking.

But too often the proclamation of the Divine Word is flat, perfunctory, and uninvolving. Why? First, lectors sometimes don't seem to understand their ministry; secondly, the assembly is unaware of its responsibilities to participate and respond during the Liturgy of the Word.

Lectors need to know that they aren't just reading, but *proclaiming*. The Word is "alive and active" — in this voice, during this moment, at this place. Training in public speaking and voice projection may help, but it's prayerful knowledge of the subject-matter that enables a reader by the grace of the Holy Spirit to stand before the assembly confident in the Lord, and to deliver a proclamation that's powerful and convincing.

Lectors, as well as homilists, should be mindful of St. Augustine's observation (*De Doctrina Christiana*) to the effect that you can't preach to people if you don't love them. And you can't love them if you don't know them. If lectors and homilists know and love the people of God — the new parishioner, the poor, the rich, the smart and educated, the less intellectually gifted and uneducated, and all in between — their communication will show it.

The assembly's role is to *actively* celebrate the liturgy. The assembly is to listen, because the Word of God comes by hearing. If they truly hear, they have the ability to respond to the Word of God "actively with full faith, hope and charity through prayer and self-giving" (*General Introduction to the Lectionary*). When the whole assembly is genuinely listening, a profound silence supervenes, a stillness which is conducive to meditation on the word spoken and received. Listening is hard work at first, but gradually people who assemble for worship come in the expectation that God is going to speak. And, with prepared lectors, He does.

In the development of its annual commemorations, the Church calendar consists of those feasts that pertain to our Lord (temporal cycle) and those that pertain to the saints (sanctoral cycle). The most important celebration of the temporal cycle of the Liturgical Year is that of Easter. In the Christmas Cycle, the two important feasts are Christmas and Epiphany.

THE ADVENT SEASON

Meaning

The liturgical year in the Roman Rite of the Catholic Church begins with the First Sunday of Advent. "Advent" is from the Latin *adventus*, meaning "coming." It's the season beginning on the Sunday nearest the feast of St. Andrew (November 30) and lasting to Christmas. The oration for the Second Sunday of Advent demonstrates its theme: "Stir us up, O Lord, to make ready for your only-begotten Son. May we be able to serve you with purity of soul through the coming of him who lives and reigns. . . ."

Advent today is simultaneously a celebration of Christ's first coming, his presence in the midst of his Church as a coming in grace today, and a looking forward to his full and final coming when he will complete his work of redemption. It's therefore a celebration of past, present, and future.

Themes of Advent

The season is to help us understand that the whole of our life must be an Advent, a vigilant awaiting of the final coming of Christ. To predispose our mind to welcome the Lord who, as we say in the Creed, will one day come to judge the living and the dead, we have to learn to recognize him as present in the events of daily life. So Advent is, so to speak, an intense training that directs us decisively toward him who already came, comes continuously, and will come at the end.

Three models can serve as spiritual "guides": a First Testament prophet of consolation, Isaiah; the immediate precursor of Christ, John the Baptist; and Jesus' Blessed Mother. Isaiah exhorted his listeners to recognize the signs of the coming of the Messiah. John the Baptist preached a baptism of conversion for the forgiveness of sins. Mary in giving her "yes" without reservation becomes a clear light for our steps and the highest model for our inspiration.

The prefaces of the Masses of Advent put forth the season's themes very well. They speak of the two comings of Christ — that he humbled himself to come among us as a man, fulfilling the plan God formed long ago, and opened for us the way to salvation. Now we watch for the day, hoping that the salvation promised us will be ours when Christ our Lord will come again in his glory. Christ's future coming was proclaimed by all the prophets. The virgin mother bore him in her womb with love beyond all telling. John the Baptist was his herald. In his love Christ has filled us with joy as we prepare to celebrate his birth, so that when he comes he may find our hearts filled with wonder and praise.

THE CHRISTMAS SEASON

The name "Christmas" comes from the Old English *Cristes-messe*, "the Mass of Christ." The exact date of Jesus' birth — day, month, year — isn't known. Why, then, did the West choose December 25th and the East January 6th? There are several theories. The best information is given by Luke 2:2, which says that Jesus' birth took place during the census under Cyrinus. Cyrinus was Publius Sulpicius Quirinius, who was governor of the province of Syria. During his administration a census took place in Judea prior to the incorporation of that kingdom into the province of Syria in A.D. 6. This census took place while Caesar Augustus was ruling the Roman Empire (30 B.C. - A.D. 14).

Most scholars today hold that the birth of Jesus was assigned the date of the winter solstice — December 25th in the Julian calendar, January 6th in the Egyptian calendar — because on this day, as the sun was in the beginning of its return to the northern skies, the pagan devotees of the god Mithra celebrated the birthday of the sun. The Roman Emperor Aurelian, on December 25th, 274 A.D., proclaimed the sun-god the principal patron of the Roman Empire and dedicated a temple to him in Rome. The Christians' choice of December 25th (*Natalis Invicti*) for the celebration of Christmas shows that the Church's purpose was to oppose a Christian feast to that of paganism's celebration of "the unconquered sun" (*Sol invictus*). The celebration of Christmas quickly became popular.

According to Matthew and Luke, Jesus was born in Bethlehem, a village in Judea about six miles south of Jerusalem, slightly to the west. Since it would have served no useful purpose for the early Christians to invent Jesus' birth in Bethlehem, we conclude that he was actually born there.

Themes of Christmas

As with Advent, the Mass prefaces of the Christmas cycle give an idea of the Church's thinking. A dominant theme is Christ the light. At Christmas a new light has dawned upon the world. Through the Feast of the Epiphany, we're again given notice that Christ is the light of the nations. God revealed in Christ His eternal plan of salvation and showed him as the light of all peoples. Now that Jesus' glory has shone among us, God has renewed humanity in his immortal image.

In the wonder of the incarnation God's eternal Word has brought to the eyes of faith a new and radiant vision of His glory. In Jesus we see our God made visible and so are caught up in the love of the God we can't see.

At Christmas, God fills our hearts with joy as we recognize in Christ the revelation of God's love. Although no eye can see Jesus' glory as God, now we see him as one like us. Christ is God's Son before all ages, yet now he's born in time. He's come to lift all things up to himself, to restore unity to creation, and to lead humankind from exile into God's heavenly kingdom.

At Christmas God has become one with human beings, and human beings have become one again with God. The eternal Word of God has taken upon himself our human weakness, giving our mortal nature immortal value. So marvelous is this oneness between God and the human race that in Christ the human race restores to itself the gift of everlasting life.

Customs

There are many happy and beautiful customs connected with Advent and Christmas. One is the *Advent wreath.* It consists essentially of four candles in a circle of cut evergreen branches. One candle is lit in each of the four weeks of Advent in preparation for Christmas. It's eternity's clock: a circle that says that in our ending is our beginning. It's also the wheel of time: The circle of evergreen branches, cut and left to wither, reveal that death and life are both of a piece. And it's a crown — the victor's garland, the sign that the race is done and the prize is won; it's the crown of us as a people, a chosen race, a royal priesthood; it's the crown of each of us as baptized individuals marked for eternity.

The use of the *crèche* (crib) in church and home derives ultimately from the grotto in Bethlehem and its reproduction in the basilica of St. Mary Major in Rome. The earliest datable Roman relief (343 A.D.) already pictures the ox and the ass, following a faulty interpretation of Isaiah 1:3, which the apocryphal Gospel of Pseudo-Matthew 15 popularized. Our oldest devotional crib is the marble group carved by Arnolfo di Cambio (d. 1302).

It was St. Francis of Assisi who really launched the popular crib devotion with his *presepio* in 1223. Promoted by the Franciscans and other religious, the custom spread widely on the continent of Europe. By the dawn of the baroque era, the crib setting had become an intricate scenic landscape, and numerous secular figures were added to those of the Holy Family, shepherds, and Magi. Crib-making developed into an important folk art, especially in Portugal, the Tyrol, and most of all in the Kingdom of the Two Sicilies. That last included Naples, and today even such a secular institution as the Metropolitan Museum of Art in New York City has an annual Christmas display of a beautiful Neapolitan *crèche*.

The home crib became popular in Catholic Europe after 1600. Except for the pietist Moravians, manger-building wasn't originally adopted by Protestants. Pre-Reformation England had had its own crib custom — baking a mince pie in an oblong manger shape to cradle an image of the Christ-child. The British Puritans, in outlawing Christmas, declared particular war on mince pie as "idolatrie in crust." Missionaries and immigrants from various European countries brought their crib customs to the Americas.

To go and see the baby in the Christmas *crèche* is the simplest prayer in the world. We can wander in, gaze, and share our thoughts like the shepherds and Magi. Or we can simply look — the prayer of "simple regard." We can do this on our feet, like the shepherds; on our knees, like the Magi; or sitting, like mother Mary.

At the crib, Mary's face has the look of a girl in the presence of an admiring lover: both vulnerable and honored, flushed with incredulous joy. In front of her new-born child, she adds to the wonder of contemplating the Christ-child all the power of her prayer before the announcing angel Gabriel: "Here I am, the Lord's servant. Let it be done to me according to your word." Mary's son later taught others to pray to the heavenly Father in almost identical words, and lived this theme through Gethsemane and Calvary.

Christmas cards are a unique form of greeting sent as an expression of good will. The first Christmas card, as now understood, is believed to have been designed in England in 1843. The practice has been followed in all English-speaking countries and is growing in many others.

The *Christmas tree* is an evergreen decorated with lights and ornaments as a part of Christmas festivities. The use of evergreen trees, wreaths, and garlands as a symbol of eternal life was an ancient custom of the Egyptians, Chinese, and Hebrews. But the modern Christmas tree originated in Germany. The main prop of a popular medieval play about Adam and Eve was a fir tree hung with apples (Paradise tree) representing the Garden of Eden. The Germans set up a "Paradise tree" in their homes on December 24, the religious feast day of Adam and Eve. They hung wafers on it, symbolizing the Eucharistic host; the hosts eventually became cookies. Candles were added as a symbol of Christ, the light of the world. By the eighteenth century the custom was widespread among the German Lutherans. It wasn't until the early nineteenth century that it was introduced into England, where it was popularized by the German Prince Albert, husband of Queen Victoria. Brought to the United States by German immigrants as early as the seventeenth century, by the nineteenth century Christmas trees were the height of fashion. They also became popular in many other countries.

The term *carol*, formerly designating a Christmas hymn of popular nature, is now used of all Christmas songs. There are almost as many definitions of "carol" as there are collections of them or books about them. Essentially, carols have religious impulses that are simple, merry, popular, and suitable for singing. Popular carols originated in Italy under the influence of St. Francis of Assisi. Most of today's well-known carols were composed since mid-nineteenth century. Though associated with the medieval French *carole*, the carol today is essentially English, representing a family of poetical and musical fixed forms. A background of folk custom can often be sensed.

At the time of the Protestant Reformation the carol fell into disfavor, mainly because it was associated with the "papist" and "superstitious" practices of "unreformed Catholicism." Nevertheless it continued to develop. And some Christmas themes found their way into broadside ballads, cheaply printed and hawked about the streets to be sung to popular tunes of the day. The purely jovial and festive side, often present in the medieval carol, continues to dominate.

During the eighteenth century the carol eked out a precarious existence. The nineteenth century rediscovered the carol and its meaning. There was a connection between the carol revival and the Oxford Movement. The latter was a group centered at Oxford University that sought a renewal of Catholic thought and practice within the Church of England in opposition to that church's Protestant tendencies. Some of the movement's followers gradually moved closer to the Roman Catholic Church. Folk songs, Protestant piety, Gothic taste, doctrinal hymns, ancient Latin song, antiquarian scholarship, and the renewal of Catholic worship all found a place in the revival of the carol that's still vigorous.

Exchanging gifts, so in harmony with the meaning of Christmas, occupies a lot of time and attention. In most parts of Europe it was the Christ Child who brought the gifts. The Eastern churches honor the gifts of the Magi at Epiphany. Appropriately, Jesus' instructions as he sent out his disciples conclude, "The gift you have received, give as a gift." Christmas gift-giving therefore simply celebrates what we should be doing all year long: giving generously of what we have received.

The gifts of consoling the weary and depressed, of encouraging the timid, of brightening the day for the unloved, of listening well to the neglected, of helping someone see through problems to possible solutions, of performing helpful duties for the disabled — the list of what we can give to the world around us (neighbors, fellow workers, parish, community, school, business) is as endless and varied as we are.

Santa Claus is in the Christian tradition. Whereas during Advent and Christmas the Church prominently puts before us the prophet Isaiah, the Virgin Mary, St. Joseph, and St. John the Baptist — as well as the coming baby Jesus, of course — in the United States the most famous person seems to be Santa Claus and, sometimes, Jesus.

In the Christian tradition, Santa's name is really Saint Nicholas. His name "Santa Claus" is after the Dutch "Sinter Claes." Probably the Bishop of Myra in Asia Minor, now Turkey, in the early fourth century, he's become the patron saint of children, of sailors (whom he reportedly saved off the coast of Lycia), of charitable fraternities and guilds, of cities such as Fribourg (in Switzerland) and Moscow, as well as such countries as Russia and Greece. Numerous surnames of people are derived from

Nicholas (for example, Nichols, Nicholson, Colson, Collins). Thousands of churches are dedicated to him.

An early story links Nicholas to the tradition of gift-giving. It's said that in his town of Myra lived a family with three daughters so poor they didn't have enough money for one dowry, so none of them could marry. The eldest volunteered to sell herself into slavery and prostitution to earn a dowry for the other two. Nicholas heard of this and anonymously sent three gifts of money to the family over three years, allowing the three daughters to marry, one after another.

The first time he did it, the money was said to have been thrown over a garden wall in a purse that landed down the daughters' chimney — creating the popular myth about Santa Claus and chimneys. Another time the purse, after being thrown over the wall, became tangled with clothes on a wash line; hence Santa's connection with Christmas stockings.

Few books received the acceptance of *A Christmas Carol* by Charles Dickens (1812-70). It immediately entered the consciousness of Christmas. Dickens' view of life was later described as "Christmas philosophy." That "philosophy," never fully elaborated, involved more than wanting the Christmas spirit to prevail throughout the year. His great attachment to Christmas, in his family as well as in his writings, contributed to his popularity. Cumulatively his books, essays, and stories about Christmas represent a celebration of Christmas attempted by no other great author, and remains in the Christmas ambience.

Santa Claus, as he's now presented in the United States and other English-speaking countries, is a symbol augmented in New York City. Two men were especially responsible. Clement Clarke Moore, a prominent Protestant New York City theologian, became famous for a little poem which he wrote for his six children. That poem, "A Visit from St. Nicholas," written in 1822, began "'Twas the night before Christmas." The second man responsible for New York City's transformation of Santa Claus was Thomas Nast, the cartoonist who illustrated Moore's poem in 1860 for *Harper's Weekly*.

By the 1870's, parents and children were writing Santa and he was writing back. One letter received a famous reply. It was a habit in the family of Dr. Philip O'Hanlon and his wife Laura that whenever they had any question of historical fact, they wrote to their favorite newspaper, the *New York Sun*. So in the Summer of 1897 their eight-year-old Virginia, with the encouragement of her parents, childishly scrawled a letter to the paper, saying: "Some of my friends say there is no Santa Claus. Please tell me the truth, is there a Santa Claus?"

A veteran editor, Francis P. Church, was assigned to answer the question. In his editorial of September 21, 1897, belief in Santa personified belief in all the intangible good things about people that really did exist but couldn't be seen. His clever editorial also typified the best of Christianity. His answer said, in part: "Yes, Virginia, there is a Santa Claus." (For further details on the customs of Christmas, see the meditation for December 25.)

CONCLUSIONS

The two main holidays that celebrate the divinity of Christ are Easter and Christmas. Two popular songs have taken Christ out of them both: "Easter Parade" and "I'm Dreaming of a White Christmas." One turns Easter into a fashion show and the other turns Christmas into a holiday about snow.

As for "White Christmas," introduced in 1940, it was, significantly, the first Christmas song to become a hit; it paved the way for such others as "Silver Bells," "Have Yourself a Merry Little Christmas," "Chestnuts Roasting on an Open Fire," "The Little Drummer Boy," and a host of other holiday perennials designed to prey upon easy emotions.

The more Christmas evolved into a public holiday, something that began to occur around the end of the nineteenth century, the more secular it had to become: United States government offices, after all, can't close in honor of what is just Jesus' birthday. This process of secularization can be expected to accelerate as millions of non-Western, non-Christian people pour into this country.

Each year the abandonment of Christ in Christmas gets worse. Department store employees are instructed not to say "Merry Christmas"; "Happy Holidays" becomes the proverbial greeting. School calendars dub Christmas vacation the "Winter Holiday"; in school, children sing songs about reindeer; the Christmas tree becomes an ersatz religious symbol; instead of B.C. and A.D., we're urged to use C.E. (Common Era) and B.C.E. (Before the Common Era). But Christians will never forget that Christmas is the story of Christ's birth.

Today the Christmas cycle ends with the octave of Epiphany (January 12). Epiphany (from the Greek *epiphaneia*, "manifestation") is one of the three principal and oldest festival days of the Christian Church (including Easter and Christmas). It commemorates (principally in the Western Church) the first manifestation of Jesus to the Gentiles, represented by the Magi, and the manifestation of his divinity as it occurred at his Baptism (especially in the Eastern Church) and at his first miracle at Cana.

The period from the end of the Christmas Cycle which ends on January 12, to Lent, and the period from Trinity Sunday to the First Sunday of Advent, are designated as "Ordinary Time," or the time through the year.

We may advantageously ask ourselves some questions that are pertinent to the seasons of Advent and Christmas. Have I become cold, indifferent, or lazy toward God and the needs of others? Am I reverent? Do I try to recognize the presence of God in the Eucharist, in the scriptures, and in other people, especially the poor? Is my life a living song of the goodness of God? Is His holiness reflected in the purity of my life — my activities, my relationships, my clothing, my decisions? Do I make room for silence and recollection in my daily life?

Am I generous in sharing my time, talents, and resources? What's the key source of power in my life: God, or myself? Do I rejoice in the light of Christ, or in the deceiving lights offered by the world? Do I let my light shine before the world for God's glory?

If in reading these materials you think that the meditations for each day are long, YOU'RE RIGHT! The reason for the length is that we hope you will be able to use a part each year — thus making these materials useful for many years.

If you find these materials helpful and to your liking, you may be happy with my *Pastoral Talks for Special Occasions* (for New Year's Day, Valentine's Day, Graduations, Civil Observances, and so forth); *God Still Speaks: Listen! - Cycle A*, or *All Things Made New - Cycle B*, or *Ode to Joy - Cycle C* (all for Sundays); or *Thirst for Life*, or *The New out of the Old*, or *Rejoicing in Hope* (all for the weekdays of Ordinary Time), or *Embrace Your Renewal* (for the weekdays of Lent), or *Life out of Death* (for the weekdays of Easter) — all published by Alba House, 2187 Victory Blvd., Staten Island, N.Y., 10314; tel. 1-800-343 ALBA (2522).

ADVENT SEASON

Monday, First Week of Advent

Is 2:1-5; Mt 8:5-11

The Joy of Advent

The Roman centurion who sought Jesus' help in today's gospel must have known that his prospects weren't good. He was a military officer of the hated occupying army in command of a "century," a company of 100 soldiers. But because the Roman legions were seldom kept at the maximum strength of 6,000 men in Our Lord's time, the century often consisted of only 50 to 60 men. The centurion, a company commander, was probably the equivalent of a captain today, though he rose from the ranks and would be considered a non-commissioned officer. The centurion was to the Roman legion what a mainspring is to a watch: the whole army depended on him.

Circumstances suggest that this particular centurion was probably in the service of Herod Antipas, the local ruler of Galilee on behalf of Rome. This incident took place in Jesus' adopted town of Capernaum in Galilee, where memories of Roman cruelty were fresh.

The centurion's dying servant would have been a non-Roman from some captured nation. Very probably he was a penniless Jew who was possibly the reason why his master came to have faith in Jesus. The centurion was a generous man, well-disposed and even loving toward the Jews: he had built a synagogue for them. And he was a humble man, coming to Jesus, a Jew, for the sake of curing his slave.

He showed his sensitivity toward the Jewish custom of not entering the home of a Gentile, which would make a Jew ritually unclean. In words we paraphrase before we receive Holy Communion, he said he wasn't worthy to have Jesus enter under his roof. Asserting his own position of authority whereby he could summon or dismiss people under him, he expressed faith that Jesus could command nature to work a cure from a distance.

The centurion's reputation as a good man wasn't unlike the tribute paid by an anonymous writer to a good soldier today. He wrote that it's the soldier, not the reporter, who has given us freedom of the press. It's the soldier, not the poet, who has given us freedom of speech. It's the soldier, not the campus organizer, who has given us freedom to demonstrate. It's the soldier who salutes the flag, who serves beneath the flag, and whose coffin is draped with the flag, who makes it possible for the protester to burn the flag.

The centurion's statement of unworthiness is the cry of every honest person before God. We hear its echo in the voices of many who lament, "I'm not strong enough in my faith. Help me!" Jesus marveled at the centurion — *marveled* at him — and expressed surprise and delight at the centurion's request. But that was nothing compared to the excitement and joy of the centurion's messengers when they returned home and found the dying servant in good health.

The Lord's words to the centurion — that he would cure his servant — set the tone for the season of Advent and describe beautifully what we prepare for in this season: the coming of the Lord to cure and to save. Unlike some who believe that the horrors around us can be solved with more policemen, larger prisons, better welfare laws, longer education, and more therapy, we Christians are committed to the idea that our current human ills require more: a savior.

In some ways, Isaiah's vision of universal peace, recorded in today's opening lines, summarize the finest hopes and ultimate goal of Isaiah. To hammer swords into plowshares and spears into sickles (v. 4) might seem to be taking recycling to extremes, but in the Iron Age in which Isaiah lived (about the eighth century B.C.) few could afford the luxury of both. Utilization of iron for weapons put arms in the hands of the masses for the first time and set off a series of large-scale folk movements. One had to decide whether the greater danger was from famine or from warfare, and live or die by the consequences of that decision. Isaiah urged his hearers to make a decision for God, and to live or die by God's aid alone.

Each passing Advent day will mark another step of joy toward the celebration of our Redeemer's birth. It's possible that along with this joy we may feel progressively more unworthy, perhaps lacking in fervor. But let's not confuse mere nervous or physical exhaustion or ordinary tiredness with genuine spiritual mediocrity or a pernicious routine that can increase its grip on the soul day by day. We can get out of any possible state of numb insensibility by making acts of faith, hope, and love, and by praying for an increase in these supernatural virtues.

Faith, humility, and refinement were united in the centurion's soul. That's why the Church commends his example to us and uses his words as preparation for receiving Jesus in Holy Communion. Jesus isn't there as a reward for the strong, but as a remedy for the weak.

To prepare for Advent, we might ask ourselves several simple questions. Are we ready to forget injuries and grudges, forgive unkind words and actions — as we would beat swords into plowshares and spears into sickles? Can we take at least a few small steps away from our fears and prejudices in the direction of Isaiah's universal vision of peace? As we come to celebrate the Advent and Christmas seasons, is there trust and hope in our approach?

If Advent is to be more than a quaint and cozy anticipation of the birth of a baby, we must believe that change can take place, that we can open ourselves more to the influence of the Lord. Using Isaiah's words as our own in this beginning of Advent, come, let's climb the Lord's mountain, that he may instruct us in his ways and we may walk in his paths.

Is 11:1-10; Lk 10:21-24

Fairy Tales, Reality, and Openness to the Spirit

Some children under ten years of age were inadvertently admitted behind the scenes in Disneyland; they saw Mickey Mouse and other Disney characters with their costume heads off. Their mother sued for damages for "trauma to her children."

Should children be told the truth about Mickey Mouse? How about Santa Claus? In a survey, 91 percent of 200 child psychologists and pediatricians advised parents to beat around the bush when pressed by children under the age of six on the question of Santa's existence.

Where does the word of God come down in the discussions about fairy tales and children? Well, the words, phrases, and images that are so familiar to us at Christmas over the years come one after the other from the scriptures, as in our reading from Isaiah today. To understand that reading, we must appreciate that God had made a promise to King David through His prophet Nathan that David's kingdom would last forever (2 S 7:8-16). But the kings descended from David were worthless, weak, and usually corrupt. By Isaiah's time (eighth century B.C.), many doubted Nathan's words.

Isaiah believed that God's promise would be kept: one day there would be another king as great as David, a man after God's own heart. To Isaiah, God had to be true to His word. The dynasty in some way would survive. The promised descendant of David would be filled with wisdom, understanding, fortitude — everything lacking in the kings after David.

For Christians, that prophecy is fulfilled in Jesus — the Christ, "the anointed one." It's upon him that Isaiah says that the spirit (*ruach*) of the Lord shall rest (v. 2). This new king will be committed to God's own moral standards. Isaiah mentions what mystical theology has come to know as the gifts of the Holy Spirit: wisdom, understanding, counsel, strength, knowledge, piety, and fear of the Lord. All of them are practical and all down to earth. There are, besides, *fruits* of the Spirit: perfections that the Holy Spirit can form in us. St. Paul listed twelve (Gal 5:22f): charity, joy, peace, patience, kindness, goodness, generosity, gentleness, faithfulness, modesty, self-control, and chastity. These have become a tradition of the Church (*Catechism of the Catholic Church*, 1832).

Isaiah is really describing the reign of the Messiah as a poetic expression of an ideal rather than a prediction of the future. The passage includes (vv. 6-9) images drawn from the garden of Eden as a dramatic symbol of the universal peace and justice of the messianic time, referred to also in today's Responsorial Psalm. That means not simply a king whose judgments won't be corrupt or based on appearances or decided by kickbacks, as with the Davidic kings, but by uprightness.

For the peace we seek, Pope John XXIII in his encyclical *Pacem in Terris* (1963) identified four important requirements: *truth, justice, love*, and *freedom*. These principles, the Pope stated, should guide actions at all levels: between individuals, within families, among associations, and at the international level.

The word of God through Jesus in today's gospel praises his heavenly Father because He has hidden from the learned and clever — like the scribes and Pharisees — the wisdom He has revealed to the merest children: people like we're all supposed to be.

Somewhere between the sandbox and the work place we often lose much of life's magic. The Society of Childlike Grown-ups has the motto, "It's Never Too Late to Have a Happy Childhood, and to Make Sure that Others Do, Too!" They consider themselves entitled to: walk in the rain, jump in mud puddles, smell flowers, blow bubbles, go barefoot, sing in the shower, have a merry heart, act silly, dance, fly kites, laugh or cry out loud, just wander around, ask lots of questions, draw and paint and color, talk with animals, trust the universe, climb trees, daydream, get excited about *everything*, be a clown, find out how things work, make up stories, make new friends, and do *anything* that brings more happiness, celebration, and life energy to all human beings of this planet.

Consider the six-year-old beautiful freckle-faced little girl, an image of innocence who was with her Mom at a shopping mall. It was pouring rain — the kind of rain that gushes over the top of rain gutters, so much in a hurry to hit the earth that it has no time to flow down the spout.

Bystanders all stood just inside the door. They waited, some patiently, others irritated because the rain messed up their hurried day. The voice of the little girl was sweet. "Mom, let's run through the rain," she said.

"What?" Mom asked.

"Let's run through the rain!" She repeated.

"No, honey. We'll wait until it slows down a bit," Mom replied.

The young child waited about another minute and repeated: "Mom, let's run through the rain."

"We'll get soaked if we do," Mom said.

"No, we won't, Mom. That's not what you said this morning," the young girl said as she tugged at her Mom's arm.

"This morning? When did I say we could run through the rain and not get wet?"

"Don't you remember? When you were talking to Daddy about his cancer, you said, 'If God can get us through this, He can get us through anything'!"

The entire crowd stopped dead silent. Mom paused. This was a moment when innocent trust can be nurtured so that it will bloom into faith.

"Honey, you're absolutely right. Let's run through the rain.

If God lets us get wet — well, maybe we just needed washing," Mom said.

Off they ran, holding their shopping bags over their heads. The bystanders all stood watching, smiling and laughing as the two darted past cars and through puddles. They got soaked. But they were followed by a few who screamed and laughed like children all the way to their cars.

Children have many gifts that adults could profit from. One is the gift of play. Kids naturally inject play into whatever they do. Another gift of children is trying. Children see the world as a place filled with new skills to master. Adults, on the other hand, often ask themselves, *Is it easy to do?* We find reasons for *not* doing something new — such as learning a foreign language or taking up a new sport.

But we shouldn't stop trying. We ought to try something new that we would love to master. We ought to let ourselves make mistakes. We don't have to be great at something to enjoy it. And we ought to offer encouragement to others when they're trying something new or difficult.

We conclude by reminding ourselves of several things. For one, humble folk are God's kind of people. Jesus the carpenter was one of them. That doesn't condemn intellectual pursuit or achievement. Far from it: intellectual pursuit is praiseworthy, and our Church community needs more of it. What Jesus is condemning is intellectual *pride* and *smugness*. He's not connecting faith and ignorance, but faith and lowliness: this consisting of simplicity, openness, and trust — the kinds of virtues we observe in a child (and in mature adults). God's revelation isn't denied to so-called "learned and clever" people — provided they're at the same time humble, open, and trusting like children.

Another conclusion is that we see the reason behind the fairy tale in Isaiah. Perhaps the calf and the young lion will never browse together. Perhaps babies shouldn't ever be allowed to play by the cobra's den. Yet the dream of universal peace and gentle trust is so wonderful that not even our fairy tales adequately measure up to it.

A third conclusion is that the world of the Messiah is still in the process of being born. His age, like the first Christmas, is a slow birthing.

The blessings of Christmas for any one of us will be in proportion to our willingness to have our eyes and ears opened to the Lord. An attitude of smug satisfaction will prevent anything new from coming into our lives. The childlikeness commended by the Lord consists in a willingness to believe there is more to see and more to hear than we have thus far seen and heard.

Wednesday, First Week of Advent

Is 25:6-10; Mt 15:29-37

Dependence: Psychologically Normal?

Frequent discussions among psychologists are along the lines of a title that was listed for a psychology conference recently: "Making People: the Normal and Abnormal in Constructions of Personhood." Concepts regarding what is normal and abnormal have a major impact on life, shaping scientific and medical research, and determining the sort of educational and other treatment people receive.

Normality has been subject to redefinition as a result of various pressures. Some therapists today are concerned with helping clients achieve independence and autonomy as qualities necessary to a normal lifestyle. Whereas at the beginning of the twentieth century psychologists could deploy only a handful of terms categorizing abnormal individuals, a recent version of their *Di-*

agnostic and Statistical Manual lists over 260 forms of mental illness.

For some therapists, dependence seems to be a putdown. They theorize that if we're financially secure and confident in the way life's going, notions of total independence are reinforced and normality is assured. If we need to be saved from anything, that idea goes, we can act in that direction ourselves without the help of religion, but with the help of scientific technology.

Much of the language of scripture must appear outlandish to some psychologists: for example, such expressions in today's reading from Isaiah as that the Lord will save us. Today's gospel miracle of the feeding of the four thousand picks up the theme of the heavenly banquet described in Isaiah. Isaiah's banquet image of a great feast for all peoples implies a guarantee of friendship and peace.

Today's gospel is set at a mountain near the shores of the Lake of Galilee. This beautiful blue lake was ringed on the western shore with a chain of little towns lying at the foot of green hills thick with woods, bright with gardens, and loud with the music of running water. There were docks and harbors, the sound of hammers as the coopers barreled fish, the noise of shipbuilders, the smoke and smell of the dye-works at Magdala, and the pottery kilns. The lakeshore towns embraced streets, villas, and amphitheaters for touring companies of actors and gladiators.

The people of the lake as Jesus knew them were a part of the variegated world balanced between East and West. Jesus met near its shores long caravans working southward across the fords of the Jordan, bands of Phoenician merchants, Roman cohorts, litters and chariots of the great, and bands of strolling players bound for the local Greek cities (the Decapolis). It's the modern world, really, with its money changers, tax collectors, market places, and unhappy rich people. Jesus in this place isn't a man retired from the world, but among people of many nations upon one of the main highways of the Roman Empire. St. Matthew speaking of the crowd glorifying the God of Israel (v. 31) shows that Jesus' audience at this time was mostly non-Jewish.

Many abnormal people were brought to Jesus (v. 30). There were the *physically* deformed: the blind, those who couldn't speak correctly, cripples, and others. The *psychologically* abnormal were, as today, less easy to spot. The least easy to spot were the *spiritually* abnormal, a category that includes all of us. We may be spiritual cripples who see the right way to go, but are incapable of getting there. Or we may be spiritually deformed. Or we may be spiritually blind, not seeing the world and other people as God sees them, which is the true reality.

Jesus was moved with pity for the crowd (v. 32). They'd been with him for three days, and now in the full heat of summer it was very oppressive in this low-lying basin surrounded by mountains. Besides, their food had by this time run out. Jesus multiplied the seven loaves and a few fish for thousands of people. The seven hampers filled with leftovers were as big as the one in which St. Paul was later let down over the wall of Damascus.

This season of Advent is a season for our recognizing how much we need the saving help of Jesus for growth into normalcy. The perfectly normal is Jesus. To the extent possible, we should imitate him. Although Samuel Johnson once observed that no person had ever become great by imitation, counterfeiting is a profitable business, as is violating copyright and patent laws. And it's possible to become great by imitating Jesus. If we do that, we're not counterfeit, or violative of copyright, or abnormally dependent — but truly normal.

This is a good time to ask, "What's abnormal in my life that needs healing?" To begin, we can imitate God's mercy as illustrated in today's gospel. We can do that in two ways. One is through the use of God's sacrament of mercy: penance, or confession. The other is in our behavior toward others. St. John Chrysostom said that nothing can make us an imitator of Jesus as much as our concern for others.

Central to our behavior toward others are the works of mercy, the possibilities of which are countless. With the so-called material works of mercy, the sick and the elderly merit special attention. Alongside these are the many works of mercy that are spiritual.

For all who seek normality through him, Jesus' heart is moved with pity now no less than on that mountain in today's gospel. He loves us and will help to cure us, if we but acknowledge our dependence on him. The result can be no less astonishment on the part of observers now than over Jesus' healings in his day, plus our much-desired normalcy.

Thursday, First Week of Advent

Is 26:1-6; Mt 7:21, 24-27

God Is... to Me

A little boy was sitting on his grandfather's lap as the older gentleman read him a story. From time to time, the boy reached up to touch his grandfather's wrinkled cheek. Alternately he stroke his own cheek, then his grandfather's again. Finally he asked, "Grandpa, did God make you?" "Yes, son," he answered, "God made me a long time ago." "Oh," the boy said, "And did God make me too?" "Yes, indeed, son," he said, "God made you just a little while ago." Feeling their respective faces again, the boy observed, "God's getting better at it, isn't he?"

God is many things to us. Today's passage from Isaiah abounds in images of God as a protector from invading armies: "strong city," "guard," "wall and rampart," "gates." Such images came naturally to a people who for much of their history were the prey of more powerful surrounding nations, and who had learned that their only defense was to trust in the Lord. Isaiah also called the Lord an eternal rock, an image familiar in the Old Testament. Jesus compared God to bread, in that He's our sustenance, and to light, inasmuch as He's our guide. Surprisingly, Jesus even compared God to a thief in the night (Mt 24:43).

Isaiah spoke from a time of crisis when Ahaz was King of Judah. Ahaz was unable to muster an army and repel an invasion from the northern kingdom of Israel. To appeal to Assyria for help would mean becoming a vassal of this foreign power. Ahaz had no choice but to trust in God.

This theme of trust in God is applicable to us all. The Lord will surround us who have faith, as He did the holy city Jerusalem, with "walls and ramparts." God is behind and before us, around us and within us, supporting us from beneath, fortifying us from above. Anyone who hears God's words and puts them into action is building on rock.

Today's gospel is the conclusion of Jesus' opening sermon, which puts forth a kind of program and has in view a new order of things. It contrasts in some ways with the first section of the Lord's Prayer. In the Lord's Prayer we pray, "hallowed be Thy name"; here (v. 21) we learn that not everybody who cries God's name from their need and emptiness is acceptable. Lip service isn't enough; we have to show some evidence of good will, too: to make some active effort. That evidence is in the way we treat our neighbor, the poor, the suffering.

In the Lord's Prayer we pray, "Thy kingdom come"; here we learn of those who will enter the kingdom. In the Lord's Prayer we ask that God's will be done; here we learn that, to enter God's kingdom, we must do God's will.

Jesus calls us to action, not mere understanding or fine words (v. 24). We can make poor choices. When hiking, we may have searched for big solid rocks as stepping stones across a gushing stream; a poor choice leaves us in rushing cold water. If we choose to invest in the wrong stock, we lose money. If we choose the wrong foods at the market, we suffer malnutrition. Spiritually, we have to choose wisely to reach out and be an image of God's love by giving alms, sharing concern, giving a needed smile, encouraging others. Many people — all of us at one time or other — confess God with our lips and deny Him with our lives. It's seldom hard to recite the creed, but it's often hard to live the Christian life. Opportunity may knock once, but temptation bangs on our door often.

In Palestine the torrential rains of the winter months — about November to March — often destroyed houses that weren't solidly built. St. Matthew's description of the inevitable winter storms is vivid, powerful, and true to reality. Jesus' illustration isn't that of a theoretician, but of a practical man, the worker in wood that he himself was. It's important for us to remember that the time of trial, the rainy season (v. 25), will come.

Jesus tells us about two houses. In one of them, the builder didn't take as much care as he should have. Perhaps he wanted to economize, or maybe he was in a hurry to finish the building. The two houses looked identical when completed, but they had very different foundations. Our life can be built safely only on the sure foundation of Jesus.

Jesus asks that we not only hear, or assent, but that we perform as well. Even non-Christian students can pass examinations with distinction in Christian doctrine; it happens all the time. Our religion isn't simply a matter of knowledge, however, but of commitment. That's possible only if we build our faith on the rock of practice, not on the sands of emotion. A good example is our Christmas season, when we contemplate the foundations of our faith and do what's necessary to act as Jesus would. Knowledge must be translated into action, theory into practice, and theology (the study of God) into theophily (the love of God).

In Isaiah, God builds the city, setting up its walls and ramparts; in the gospel we build the house solidly, setting it on rock.

The Jewish Scripture in this instance appears as the messenger of faith; the New Testament stresses action.

It's said that a tree planted in a rain forest isn't forced to send its roots down in search of water; because of that, it's toppled easily by the mildest of winds. A mesquite tree in a dry desert, on the other hand, is forced to send its roots thirty feet or more in search of the cool waters that feed it, thereby anchoring it for the worst disaster.

Let's pray that we will be like the wise person in today's gospel who built his house upon rock. Then when the rains of temptation fall, and the floods of evil rise, and the winds of suffering and doubt blow and buffet our spiritual house, neither we nor our house will fall.

Friday, First Week of Advent

Is 29:17-24; Mt 9:27-31

Strong Faith in Action

A story is told about an aerial gymnast who was billed as Zumbrati the Magnificent. He was in the habit of walking a tightrope across Niagara Falls. On one occasion, conditions were less than ideal: It was a windy day and the performer was thankful to have made it safely across.

One of those waiting to congratulate him was a man with a wheelbarrow. "I believe that you could walk across on that tight rope pushing this wheelbarrow," the man told him.

Zumbrati shook his head and said he felt lucky to have accomplished the feat without a wheelbarrow. The man persisted: "I believe that you can do it!"

The aerialist graciously declined, but the man kept after him. Finally, the performer said, "You really do believe in me, don't you?"

"Oh, I do," the man assured him.

"Okay," Zumbrati replied. "Get in the wheelbarrow."

That's the kind of profound faith possessed by Isaiah in today's first reading and the two blind men in the gospel. Isaiah's prophecy of salvation speaks of a new age, the age of the Messiah. The poor and lowly will be made happy, the tyrants and the arrogant will be removed, and those who cheat and ruin their neighbors will be overcome. The blind will receive sight and insight. The deaf will hear and listen with a receptive ear to the word of God. The meek and the poor will be raised up and acknowledge God's holiness.

This turning upside-down of every aspect of the world would become a key element in the gospel, expressed early on in Mary's *Magnificat*: "He casts down the mighty from their thrones and raises up the lowly."

Yet, as we read Isaiah, we can't help wondering if his poetic sense had run ahead of his common sense. Isaiah stated that in "a very little while" all the misery would cease. We're still waiting. Perhaps his description of physical transformation is symbolic of a new spiritual condition.

Signs of the dawning of a new age are evident in today's gospel passage, too. Something of the impression of unrealistic poetry in Isaiah seems to shine forth in this gospel. Jesus' healing of the two blind men was a response to their faith and pointed beyond their gaining physical sight to their spiritual insight.

The Old Testament had offered several notable views of blindness — blindness as a blemish that disqualifies a person from Temple service (Lv 21:18-21; 2 S 5:9); that a blind person is groping and incompetent (Is 59:10; Dt 28:29); that God punishes sinners by blinding them or their animals (Zp 1:17; Zc 12:4); compassion for the blind is a duty (Lv 19:14; Dt 27:18).

In the New Testament, Jesus heals the blind and disputes the Old Testament connection between blindness and sin (Jn 9:3). In the Christian tradition, Louis Braille, blind and poor, taught by a local priest, in 1824 invented a raised code that enabled the blind to be literate. His codes exist for most of the world's languages, as well as for music, mathematics, and scientific and computer notation. In many instances, however, the blind still have to fight attitudes dating back to Leviticus prohibitions. Issues faced by blind congregants range from getting to church (because public transportation is often not available on Sundays) to not being asked to take leadership roles.

In today's gospel, Jesus asked the blind men if they were confident that he could give them their sight. They answered, "Yes, Lord!" At that he told them that it was *because of their faith* that they were being cured, and he gently and lovingly *touched* their eyes.

The profound mysteries of touch emerge from the skin, arguably our most essential source of sensory stimulation. If we took off our skin and laid it flat, it would cover an area of about 21 square feet, making it by far the body's largest organ. We can live without seeing or hearing — in fact, without any of our other senses — but babies born without effective nerve connections between skin and brain can fail to thrive.

Laboratory experiments decades ago, now considered unethical, kept baby monkeys from being touched by their mothers. It made no difference that the babies could see, hear, and smell their mothers; without touching, the babies became apathetic and failed to progress. They threw themselves prone on the floor, crying and grimacing all the time, or huddled against a wall, rocking back and forth with their hands over their heads or faces.

For humans, too, insufficient touching in early years can have lifelong results. Premature babies who are touched and held show faster progress than those who aren't. In touching cultures, adult aggression is low, whereas in cultures where touch is limited, adult aggression is high.

That touch of Jesus to the blind men was precious.

After the cure of the blind men, we might expect that a party would be given for the entire village to celebrate. But the opposite took place: Jesus warned the two to see to it that no one knew of it — he didn't want his miracles to turn into a circus in which his personal concern was lost in feverish excitement. There was also, of course, the fact that he didn't want to reveal himself as the Messiah to people who had a complete misunderstanding of what that meant.

Today, there has been phenomenal scientific progress in the areas of heart disease, cancer, tuberculosis, polio, and leprosy. But many of these discoveries haven't reached out sufficiently, and there are many deaf people, many blind. If more of our resources were allocated to research into diseases instead of to luxuries and weaponry, many more would be cured; we would learn to deal with natural disasters; we wouldn't waste food and water in one part of our planet while millions were starving or dying of hunger and thirst in another.

A young university student once came to a famous theologian to lament that the secular acids of his university education had eroded his faith; he asked for some books to help him regain his faith. Instead of the books, the theologian gave him what, at first glance, might seem to be an odd piece of advice: "Go out and join a group of Christians who help the poor."

There's a deep issue behind that advice. Those who serve the poor in the name of Jesus interpret the scriptures not by reading commentaries but by doing what the gospel demands. Merely to read the Bible is like reading the score of a symphony and never listening to the music.

Jesus can help us only when we confess full faith in him — get into his wheelbarrow — and allow him to touch us where we're weak and in need. The stronger our faith in Jesus, the more urgent is his longing to cure us and transform our lives. Jesus came, after all, to seek those who are lost. We should recognize, as today's Responsorial Psalm puts it, that "the Lord is my light and my salvation." We can neither gloss over the problems of our society nor sit back and wait for the Messiah to cure them. All of Christian experience shows that God redeems and changes our world through disciples who work to make a difference — who use their minds, hearts, and talents to cooperate in the transformation of the world. One consequence will be optimism: the certainty that, in the end, things will go well.

Let's own up to our areas of spiritual blindness and expose them to Jesus' healing touch. Jesus says to us, as to the blind men, that it's because of our faith that wonderful things can be done.

Saturday, First Week of Advent

Is 30:19-21, 23-26; Mt 9:35-10:1, 6-8

Gift Giving

Between now and Christmas, gift-giving will occupy a lot of time and attention. Often that time and attention goes to what to give to mom, dad, little Joey, or Auntie Mae from the many choices we see advertised. Appropriately, Our Lord's instructions as he sends out his disciples conclude by saying that the gift we've received we're to give as a gift. Christmas gift-giving for Christians celebrates what we should be doing all year long: giving generously of what we have received.

Today's first reading is overwhelming, but consoling, as Isaiah speaks of the abundance of God's gifts. Isaiah's prophecy seems more adventurous than today's excerpt from St. Matthew.

Isaiah's vision sweeps universally across high mountains and lofty hills, across the heavens where "the light of the moon will be like that of the sun, and the light of the sun will be seven times greater." Jesus' words are less poetically expansive. He sent forth his Twelve to continue his works of mercy.

The gift of consoling the weary and depressed, of encouraging the timid, of brightening the day for the unloved, of listening well to the neglected, of helping someone see through problems to possible solutions, of performing helpful duties for the disabled — the list of what we can give to the world around us (family, relatives, neighbors, fellow workers, parish, community, school, business) is endless and varied.

The history of the Church shows us how she has been attentive to the service of the sick. She has had champions of charity, like John of God, Camillus de Lellis, Vincent de Paul, and an enormous army, especially of women. The Church has always been in the vanguard of everything that has occurred in the world of health. When there has been an epidemic, the Church has been there. The Church inherited this capacity of mercy from Jesus.

Pope John Paul II was a champion of giving to the world of the sick. When his health was strong, he gave encouragement with his word, and when he became ill he gave an example. He published a document, *Salvifici Doloris*, dedicated especially to pain, suffering, and the meaning of human suffering. He also instituted the Pontifical Council for Health Care Workers, and mediated the World's Day of the Sick, observed every year on February 11th.

Sickness is bad, but can be good in the end if a person grows in the way he sees his sickness. If a person rebels against it — the first human reaction — it's an evil. But if he moves toward acceptance, and adds love to his illness, in the end it's a good thing: the face of God comes closer.

Life is difficult. It's predicted that the illness of the future will be depression. Depression is now the fifth major cause of absence from work. In ten years, it will be the third cause.

For these new situations, a Mother Teresa isn't enough. John of God was a revolutionary, the "inventor of the modern hospital," whose great sensitivity for God made him see the sick person as his neighbor. In our world, in which medicine is being revolutionized, a new culture is needed.

Matthew, though, in today's gospel confines the apostolate of the Twelve to "the lost sheep of the house of Israel." This was in keeping with God's promises to the Patriarchs. Although Jesus worked mainly with the house of Israel, he was continually giving hints and signals of his heart's desire to embrace the world. Indeed, after his Resurrection he would instruct the Apostles to preach the gospel to all nations.

Jesus was no less adventurous than Isaiah. More than anything else, however, his compliance to the will of his heavenly Father meant that he followed the slow process of human development. That slow process means that change proceeds first within the individual, the family and the neighborhood, and only after a long time reaches out to the universe.

Today's portion of Isaiah (v. 21) says that when you turn to the right or to the left, and you hear that this is the way, walk in it. The song boasts, "I did it my way." The Bible is the record of a people who constantly did things their own way, in defiance of God's commandments. To them, and to us, Isaiah proclaims uncompromisingly, "*This* is the way."

One must, however, use discretion in listening to advice, as the story of the two tramps illustrates. They were discussing the reasons they became tramps. "I'm the fellow who never listened to anybody," said the first. "Shake hands, partner," said the second. "I'm the man who followed everybody's advice."

One of the greatest gifts God can give us is a clear view of the road that leads to Him and the opportunity to rely on someone who will help us to recover from wrong turnings. Many times in the course of their history the Hebrews strayed from the right path because they had no true guides. That's how God finds His people to be like sheep without a shepherd, as in today's gospel.

Jesus is the Good Shepherd proclaimed by the prophets. He knows each one of his sheep and calls them by name. Yes, Jesus knows us personally — calls us, seeks us, heals us. We're not submerged in a huge mass of nameless humanity: to him each of us is unique. Jesus has left good shepherds in his Church, too — the Pope, bishops, priests, deacons, lay leaders. Every Christian should be a good shepherd to his fellows, especially by means of example, prayer, and fraternal correction.

Fraternal correction is one of the greatest gifts we can give to anybody. The faults of others, like our own, may be habitual. *Receiving* such a correction *often* hurts, but *giving the gift* of fraternal correction is *almost always* hard. Among the excuses we make for putting it off is the fear of offending the person we have to warn. It seems paradoxical to think that a doctor would ever fail to tell a patient that if he wants to be cured he has to undergo a painful operation, and yet we can be reluctant to tell people that the health of their soul is at risk.

Whenever we give a fraternal correction we have to possess a series of other virtues, too, beginning with true charity. There's also humility, which teaches us to find the right words and to know how not to cause offence; we remember that we ourselves often need precisely the same kind of gift. Giving fraternal correction needs prudence, too, to lead us to give the warning promptly and at the most opportune moment.

When should we give fraternal correction? When it will benefit the other person and the community; at a time that will maximize the ability of both parties to listen; when there will be enough time for dialogue — and *not* when one is angry or frustrated.

How should we confront? Be direct and state the issue(s) succinctly. Rather than making generalized statements, indicate specific behavior. Be honest, but compassionate. Avoid "old dirt."

When possible, use objective facts. Don't interpret behavior (for example, saying "this is why you did this"). And, most important, be prepared to be confronted in return.

The role of a good shepherd requires, in addition, much love and a great deal of patience, courage, and meekness, as well as quickness of mind and a great sense of responsibility. St. Thomas of Villanueva said that the good shepherd must fulfill four conditions. First is love — this was the first virtue Our Lord demanded of Peter before he made him shepherd of the flock. Secondly, the good shepherd needs to be watchful. Third, essential also is true, proper, and appropriate doctrine, which will provide people with the food that will enable them to reach salvation. Fourth and lastly, to be a good shepherd requires integrity of one's own life.

We all need good shepherds to guide our soul: spiritual directors. They're called "director" because their purpose is to help us discern the way we should go in order best to follow God's call. The spiritual director helps us understand our journey by sharing insights, helpful ideas, and knowledge of the spiritual life. Spiritual directors are experienced in the ups and downs of spiritual practices. They're not necessarily priests, but will have some knowledge of theology and spirituality as well as counseling. A confessor isn't necessarily a spiritual director: the roles, though distinct, may overlap.

A ship with a good pilot arrives safely in port; a guide is necessary to climb a mountain without difficulty. If you meditate on the word "guidance," you see "dance" at the end of the word. Doing God's will is a lot like dancing. When two people in a dance both try to "do it my way," everything is uncomfortable and jerky. When one person relaxes and lets the other lead, both flow with the music as one body, moving beautifully. The dance takes surrender, willingness, and attentiveness from one person and gentle guidance from the other. If you look again at the word "guidance," you can think of "G" for God, followed by "u" and "i." God, "you," and "I" dance. If we think of it this way, we're ready to accept the gift of God leading.

Monday, Second Week of Advent

Is 35:1-10; Lk 5:17-26

The Impressiveness of Forgiving Sin

Home living in the Holy Land in the time of Jesus was more casual than in many places today. The houses were open to the street, and anyone who wanted to gather around the doorway or even to enter the house was free to do so. Every house also had a flat roof to which people could go for rest, for taking the sun, and to get away from it all in the cool of the evening. To that roof was a stairway from the outside. So to avoid the crowd around Jesus, the four men who brought the paralyzed man could easily bring him up the outside stairway to the roof, remove some of the roof tiles, and lower him in front of Jesus.

The paralyzed man's friends' determination wasn't stopped by risking the use of the roof nor by hearing complaints from the crowd because of the interruption. Their deep concern for their friend can be a model for the Christian response to those who are helpless, confined, hopeless. Our Lord was impressed by the decisiveness, skill, and concern of those four friends who didn't defer their supplication for a more convenient occasion: they didn't know when Jesus would be passing that way again. We don't know what Jesus was discussing. When it happened, though, Jesus abruptly stopped the discussion and gave this new group his undivided attention.

The men who brought the paralyzed man, as well as the man

himself and the others present, believed that a person's sickness, particularly a long sickness like this paralysis, was brought on by sin. The Pharisees and other teachers of the Mosaic Law from every village of Galilee and from as far away as Judea and Jerusalem were there to see to it that Jesus adhered to that "orthodox" belief. By now they had reason to suspect him but, provided that he serve their interests, why not profit from his reputation?

Some health care professionals speak of the miracles they witness in the care of the dying who are beyond all hope of medical care. By miracles they don't mean cures, however: They mean wonders of the human spirit. They see families split for decades come together to express love and regret. They see forgiveness that can be described as only heavenly. They see courage in patients whose bodies are battered beyond recognition by a cruel disease. Most of all, in the middle of it they see joy — joy in the celebration of life in the face of death, joy in the confidence of a better world to come, joy in the last touches of love from people who have shared their life here on earth.

Though the paralyzed man's friends were seeking a true miracle cure, Jesus' first words to the man were the very pitying, kindly, and astounding "your sins are forgiven" (v. 20). That grace was the sick man's reward for having allowed himself to be helped; directly he experienced a joy such as he had never before imagined.

Jesus still gives his words of forgiveness to all who want them. But when he said them then, the religious representatives among his listeners judged him to be uttering blasphemy because, they said, only God can forgive sins. And they were right: people can forgive the wrongs done them, but only God can forgive sins.

Hence Jesus' question: "Which is easier, to say 'Your sins are forgiven,' or to say, 'Rise and walk'?" Then, seeing *their* faith, Jesus *cured the paralyzed man.* After Jesus cured the man of his sins, to prove his ability to forgive sin he cured his physical illness. Jesus' action with this man was a true miracle. This is the only time in the gospels that we read of an adult who is healed because of the faith of others.

If Jesus had referred to himself as God, he would have been killed on the spot for blasphemy. As it was, he attributed to himself a controversial figure of speech from the Book of Daniel (7:13): that he was the "Son of Man" (or "son of humanity"). If his audience — especially the educated members — knew their scriptures as well as they should, they knew that he was referring to himself in the very special way of messiahship meant by the ancient prophet Daniel. But they couldn't do a thing about Jesus' application of that phrase to himself.

What struck the audience wasn't the forgiveness of sins (any charlatan could, after all, say he was forgiving sin, since much sin is invisible), but that this man whom in this little town they knew to have been paralyzed for a long time was now able to walk. They were impressed by the wrong thing: the material more than the spiritual.

There are applications of today's gospel to our lives. One is that during these days of Advent we should get ready to receive Jesus in a new way when Christmas comes. Another application is that we, any more than Jesus, can't expect that any good we do will receive a reward in this life: he went about doing good, and he was persecuted for it.

Then, too, if in those days people were perhaps overconscious of sin, we in our time are underconscious of it. Instead of calling wrong actions sins, we call them sociological aberrations, or psychological abnormalities, or problems from childhood, instead of what they really are — disturbances of the order between ourselves and God.

Also, we, unlike Jesus' audience, should be impressed by the right things. We're impressed, for example, by the fact that we can go to an airport and within a very short time be thousands of miles away. We're impressed by being able to press a button and see and hear something that's taking place on the other side of the planet. That's good and right, but many of the important things that should most impress us are the things that we can't sense — like the forgiveness of sin.

And lastly, like those who brought the paralyzed man to Jesus, we ought to realize that our faith can help others, and others' faith can help us: We're united in Jesus' mystical body. As Jesus showed in his conduct with the paralyzed man, our apostolate can't be confined only to people's souls. It requires that we be anxious to help others in all areas of their lives. It requires that we take seriously the social sins of today's world and seek the full dignity of all human beings.

Tuesday, Second Week of Advent

Is 40:1-11; Mt 18:12-14

The Value of the Lost Sheep in Each of Us

Our sun is but a medium-sized star. It's located in the outer suburbs of the Milky Way galaxy — which is a great swirling disk made up of 100 billion stars. That's *almost seventeen stars* for every man, woman, and child on Earth.

Recognizing that stars are in themselves suns, it's natural to ask whether any of them have planets going around them in the same way that our sun has Earth. The answer is that they do. About 30 planets going round other stars have been detected thus far, and more are likely yet to be discovered.

There are also other galaxies — 100 billion of them. That makes *more than sixteen galaxies* for every man, woman, and child now on Earth. Adding together all the stars of all the galaxies, the total number in the universe is approximately the same as the number of grains of sand in a seashore sandcastle five miles high by five miles wide by five miles long. Some galaxies lie so far from us that it takes almost 12 billion years for their light to reach us — light traveling at 186,000 miles (300,000 kilometers) per second.

So are we human beings on planet Earth not important? "Importance" is a slippery concept. It derives its significance from its context. For example, physically the sun is more important than we are. We go around it, it doesn't go around us; and whereas our absence would make no difference to the sun, without the sun we would die.

But if you don't *know* you're important, what's the point? And, of course, the sun doesn't know that it's important. In fact, the sun doesn't know anything: it's not conscious. It's on the notion of *consciousness* — the ability to be aware, and to have thoughts and feelings — that the whole understanding of what is and isn't important turns. We don't know much about the nature of consciousness; it appears to have something to do with the complexity of the brain. Our brain is admittedly not big on the astronomical scale, but it's probably one of the most complex and important structures to be found anywhere in the universe.

If size is to be discounted in favor of consciousness, then it's perhaps not so absurd to believe that God would take a special interest in human beings. Indeed, the chances of life forms as advanced as ourselves emerging might have happened only once in the history of the entire universe.

A full human life requires some understanding of where we are, how we got here, why we're here. The vastness of the universe says something about the vastness of the divine. We've discovered in this vastness the splendor out of which we came. We try to look out to the depths of the universe as well as into the depths of our soul.

Today's readings from both Isaiah and St. Matthew are about

our value in God's sight. Chapters 40-55 of the book of Isaiah include some of the noblest of the religious ideals to be found in the entire Jewish Scriptures. To answer his people's crisis of faith, Isaiah reminds them that their God is no mere national god but a cosmic god who puts the stars in their places. He gives strength to the powerless. Those who wait for God with trust will fly with wings like eagles.

Today's portion is the part that's most beautifully set to music by Handel in his *Messiah*. It draws a contrast between human fickleness and the constancy of God. It also presents a vision of what can happen for those who live by God's word. It was written when the people of Israel were about to be set free from their Babylonian captivity. To capture the joy and excitement of the time, the sacred writer tried to rekindle the vision of the great events of the Exodus from Egypt.

The climax is God as both powerful conquering hero and gentle shepherd-king who is close to His people (v. 10f.), a familiar figure to the ancient Jews. One of the most moving modern uses of this passage was Martin Luther King's "I Have a Dream" speech, pleading for freedom and equality for all forgotten peoples, a true messianic expectation.

Matthew's gospel picks up the shepherd image to describe the compassion of God, who searches out those people who stray. "Lost and Found" departments at churches, railroad stations, and schools are filled with all sorts of things — sunglasses, sweaters, bracelets, wrist watches. Their owners can usually replace them with others. To shepherds, though, their lost sheep are irreplaceable. Each one that strays has to be found.

God's success in finding lost sheep is not automatic — if He succeeds in finding one lost sheep, the gospel says, He rejoices more over it than over ninety-nine that didn't stray. His joy is sure because it's God's wish that not one of His valuable "little ones" be lost. This kind of joy in God (vv. 13f.) is based on an analogy with joy among human beings, with whom the greater the preceding sorrow, the greater the subsequent joy. The joy of a mother over the recovered health of a sick child is greater than her joy would be if the child had never been sick.

The lost in our society are obvious: the homeless, the street people (including children), the abused, the abandoned, the unemployed, the victims of greed, those caught between opposing factions, the starving, the poor. God's zeal in seeking even one soul that goes astray shows the great value of the human person in God's eyes.

Would that we shared God's vision of the value of the person, especially in our views on abortion, in our conduct in helping the destitute, in our concern for the lonely elderly, and in many other ways at our doorstep. One of the needs always at our doorstep is Jesus' radical teaching on the forgiveness of the sheep who have strayed. Forgiveness is the final form of love, wholehearted forgiveness so loving that it's God-like.

In each one of us, there's a hidden part that's lost. The lost sheep is that buried, secluded, or forgotten part that we might want to hide. When we allow the Good Shepherd to find that lost part, it will be His instrument for transforming our entire existence. If that "lost sheep" in us wandered away out of fright or out of simple neglect, it will be found by tender concern. If it was lost through sin, it can be brought back through forgiveness.

Every time we receive the words of absolution, the Church rejoices and is enriched, because every absolution sends blessings which resound through the whole Communion of Saints. There's no sin, not even the most intimate and secret one, that exclusively concerns the sheep who has been guilty of it.

Advent is the time to realize the high value of ourselves and other people, and to rediscover the lost sheep in ourselves as well as in others.

Wednesday, Second Week of Advent

Is 40:25-31; Mt 11:28-30

Soaring with Eagles' Wings

On a windy Spring day, children were having fun flying their kites. Multicolored creations of varying shapes and sizes filled the skies like beautiful birds, darting and dancing in the heady atmosphere.

As the strong winds gusted against the kites, a string kept them in check. The kites rose against the wind to achieve great heights. They shook and pulled, but the restraining string and the long tail kept them in tow, facing upward and against the wind. As the kites struggled and trembled against the string, they seemed to say, "Let me go! I want to be free!"

Finally, one of the kites succeeded in breaking loose. Yet its freedom from restraint put it at the mercy of an unsympathetic breeze. It fluttered ungracefully to the ground and landed in a tangled mass of weeds. It was "free at last" — free to lie powerless in the dirt, to be blown helplessly along the ground, and to lodge lifeless against the first obstruction it hit.

In the face of problems, we look to hope of liberation. That's what Isaiah and Jesus are talking about today. In the prophet Isaiah, God, having revealed Himself as Creator and almighty, addressed the Israelites who had lost hope in their exile. God hadn't forgotten them, said Isaiah, and if they remained faithful to God they would be renewed.

If we find ourselves seemingly without hope, let's think of the improbabilities of life itself. How staggeringly improbable we are! First is the fact of existence itself. No theory of the origin of our universe can tell us why creation itself occurred. We have no idea why there is something rather than nothing.

Altering any of the universe's fundamental parameters would have radically altered reality. For example, if the cosmos had been slightly more dense at its beginning, it would have quickly collapsed into a black hole. A smidgen less dense, and it would have flown apart so fast that there would have been no chance for stars, galaxies, and planets to form. Cosmologists sometimes call this the fine-tuning problem or, more colorfully, the Goldilocks dilemma.

The next improbability is life itself. Life is mysterious. No scientific theory tells us why life appeared on earth in the first place, or whether it was a once-in-eternity fluke. Once life on earth started, many scientists have contended, it was only a matter of time before natural selection produced a species as intelligent as *Homo sapiens*: us. But for more than 80 percent of life's 3.5-billion-year history, the earth's biota consisted entirely of single-celled organisms, like bacteria and algae. Not even the simplest multicellular organisms were inevitable. So how did something — intelligent beings — come from nothing?

Well, just the same, here we are! By far the greatest gift that can be bestowed on us is to see — really *see* — all that's *right* with the world. Just as believers in a beneficent deity are haunted by the problem of natural evil, so atheists, pessimists, and nihilists should be haunted by the problem of friendship, love, beauty, truth, humor, compassion, and fun. (Never forget the fun!)

What's definitely right with the world is the existence of people — even with their defects. Whenever we hope in people, we make their burden light. If we sense that someone has great hopes in us, we're buoyed up. We feel that we can, as Isaiah promised, soar as with eagle's wings! The eagle has the unique ability to lock its wing joints and soar effortlessly on an updraft. Yet hopes in people have their risks. But look at the turtle: he makes progress only when he sticks his neck out. Hopes have high stakes and risk everything for a future that remains unknown.

Risking to put our hopes in people and bonding with them in love brings excitement and adventure; it removes the danger of monotony. In such cases, we run and don't grow weary: in the notion of Isaiah we soar as with eagle's wings.

And Jesus offers restoration to all wearied and burdened people who come to him (v. 28). The word "restaurant," a French word that comes from the Latin *restaurare*, to restore to or to put back into an original state, is said to originate with that beautiful direction of Jesus.

Most often when we think of refreshment we mean having a good cup of tea, a cold drink, a shower, or sharing dinner with friends, or a delightful concert, or seeing a play — all of which we call "refreshing." Most of these are the kinds of refreshment that come quickly and predictably. The refreshment that the Lord offers, however, is the result of a life of persistence in faith and hope and in the effort to practice love.

The heart of Jesus' message is "Come to me" — a call to a personal relationship. The shift from the Pharisees' "keep the law" to Jesus' "come to me" is a significant one. A religion which is experienced only as an adherence to impersonal legalistic norms and not as a joyful life-giving relationship with the author of life is false. In coming to the person of Jesus, we discover that, like a kite or an eagle in an updraft, we're liberated.

Jesus invites us all to take his yoke upon our shoulders (v. 29). The yoke was the fitted wood collar placed on the neck of an ox pulling a plow. Jesus the carpenter had made some. They were custom-fitted so they wouldn't chafe or bruise the neck of the much-needed and very precious ox. God's yoke is custom-made to fit individually the needs and abilities of each of us whom He invites to wear it.

We sometimes hear, "Nobody ever said it was easy to be a Catholic." But Jesus said, "My yoke is easy and my burden light." Love makes every burden light (v. 30). You remember the story of the small boy appearing out of a snowstorm with a still smaller boy on his back. When a compassionate adult observed, "That's a heavy load for you to be carrying," his answer was, "He ain't heavy, mister, he's my brother."

Christmas, and the days of Advent in preparation for it, enable us to renew our hope in Jesus. By attending to God's will, not only will our yoke be easy and our burden light, but, as Isaiah points out, we will soar as with eagle's wings.

Thursday, Second Week of Advent

Is 41:13-20; Mt 11:11-15

The Nature of True Greatness

Today's reading from Isaiah begins with a fiery judgment on Israel's enemies; its second part is a song of exquisite literary beauty on behalf of the poor and needy — those who, in a parched land, search for water with gasping dry tongues. Metaphorically in ways that apply to our Advent season of preparation for Christmas, Isaiah's God doesn't answer with words, but with actions of wondrous magnitude: rivers flowing atop mountains and in desert valleys, and sacred trees of paradise. God's redemptive acts bring a new creation.

The New Dispensation, in which every disciple of Christ is mystically united with the Son of God, is so far superior to the Old that, as Jesus said, even the least in the kingdom of heaven is greater than John the Baptist, the great prophet of the Old Dispensation. Jesus also tells us, however, that no one has ever arisen greater than John the Baptist. John's greatness consisted in many things. He was, for one thing, a wonderful witness to Jesus. So good was this ascetical man, this humble man, this man of courage, that people left comfortable cities like Jerusalem to go out into the desert to listen to him.

That desert in which he preached was one of the most abandoned places in the world. Its deep gulches, arid limestone soil, and rocky precipices looked so warped and twisted that they stirred nightmarish images. Its days were unbearably hot, its nights terribly cold. Yet the ancient Israelites often romanticized the desert. There they had wandered as a rebellious people and there in later centuries they had come to idealize the desert as being the place when they were closest to the Lord.

Some aspects of the Baptist caused a number of people to think that he was the Messiah: his remarkable austerity which struck the imagination, the suddenness of his appearance, his mighty voice which shook the people from their listlessness, and the fact that there had been no prophet for about 400 years. John's self-sacrificing way of life resulted in a piercing eye, a majesty of bearing, and a voice of authority — all with a touching humility.

John's mission was to straighten out the crooked paths of human hearts and level the valleys and hills of people's selfishness to prepare them for Jesus. He did that at great cost to himself. When, for example, the Baptist's disciples John and Andrew heard the names of the passing one — Lamb, Rabbi, Messiah — they wanted to follow him. Although one of the Baptist's many good qualities was his complete lack of jealousy, he must have felt terribly lonely and futile as he watched his companions fade into the distance. His final cost would be the degradation of being beheaded.

With conviction and enthusiasm for his message, John preached repentance. Repentance signifies not regret for the past or the performance of "penance," but rather a new outlook on life in keeping with the will of God. John himself was a good model for what he preached. Although some people saw him as being so great as to be Elijah the prophet come back to life, for preaching God's word Herod had John imprisoned. From jail he sent a delegation to Jesus to get a handle on the truth of his mission. John's prayer to Jesus was, in the words of St. Richard of

Chichester adopted by the show *Jesus Christ, Superstar*, "to see you more clearly, to love you more dearly, to follow you more nearly."

Many people seem to believe that some persons are *born* to be great. The truth is that people *become* great. Except for concentrated interest, enthusiasm, and determination, great people are not from the beginning superior to those who don't become great. It starts with wanting to be the best you can.

Whereas the usual associations with the concept of greatness are power, prestige, and fame, Ben Franklin had another idea. In 1729 he wrote: "If we were as industrious to become good as to make ourselves great, we should become really great by being good.... But it is a grand mistake to think of being great without goodness. And I pronounce it as certain, that there was never yet a truly great person who was not at the same time truly virtuous."

When we see how the media and popular opinion in general dote on every action of famous people in politics, business, the arts, and sports, we may have doubts about the worth of unsung lives. Yet a tough demand of faith is that we look to the interior of human beings and judge by standards for true greatness presented there. Jesus underlines this when he calls "blessed" the poor and those who mourn. The spirit of Advent, counter to what's going on in our media and in our streets this time of year, is one of quiet waiting for the rebirth of the Lord through us in our world.

Advent is an especially good time to ask ourselves how much we struggle against our own passions, defects, sins, and bad inclinations. Our Lord asks us to keep up our struggle through the whole of our life, but most particularly during those liturgical seasons when he seems to draw especially close to us in his sacred humanity. Our struggle concerns itself with the way we live charity, making real efforts to be friendly, good-tempered, and considerate to the people around us; with offering our work to God and then doing it as well as we can; in taking all the appropriate steps to make sure that our personal spiritual development doesn't stagnate; in smiling at whomever needs cheering up, even when there's sorrow in our heart; and in devoting the necessary time to prayer.

On the way that leads to God, to sleep is to die. As with freezing in the snow, the approach of death has no special feel. We continue to struggle. As St. John Chrysostom reminded us, in a battle it's only the ones who don't fight who are never wounded.

We can't expect to be victorious all the time. With patience and humility, we can start all over again, even though we see no results. The scientist goes back over his calculations time after time and renews his experiments by modifying them until he has found the object of his research. The writer shapes and reshapes his sentences. The sculptor breaks one rough model after another until he succeeds in giving birth to his vision. All human "creations" are the result of untiring new beginnings.

As we prepare for Christmas, let's recognize John the Baptist as the classic Advent figure, representing as he does the importance of preparation, the joy of witnessing to the Good News, and the nature of true greatness.

Friday, Second Week of Advent

Is 48:17-19; Mt 11:16-19

Cafeteria Catholics

For defense, ancient cities needed surrounding walls. Because the walls were expensive to build, maintain, and defend, the walls and the cities they enclosed were kept as small as possible. So the streets were narrow and the houses crowded together. The only open spaces were the shopping centers, so these naturally served as the children's playgrounds.

It was to such a situation that Jesus referred in today's gospel. He was continuing to teach about the question of his identity put by John the Baptist's messengers, and giving his testimony in favor of John. The children in his story were playing "wedding" and "funeral." Those who played the flute expected their playmates to dance as at a wedding; those who sang a dirge expected a make-believe funeral. But some of the children were so disagreeable that they found fault with their companions *whatever* game they proposed.

At this point, Jesus was referring to some of the differences between himself and John the Baptist. Some sour grown-ups were criticizing those who were "piping" the celebratory light yoke of Jesus, while others were disagreeing with the more severe message of John. They criticized Jesus for encouraging his followers to joyfully eat and drink, John for encouraging his followers to stern fasting.

We still have critics like that. Nothing the Church does will satisfy some. Inside the Church, they're called "cafeteria Catholics": They pick and choose the game they play. If they like the teachings of Jesus' Church on a specific issue, they will accept them; if not, they won't. In France, a formerly Catholic country, polls show that only 13 percent of the populace believes that it's necessary to believe in God to be moral, whereas in the United States that belief is 58 percent. In the religious controversies between liberals and conservatives, some liberals wear T-shirts declaring, "So Many Right-Wing Christians; So Few Lions."

If we accept Jesus as the Son of God and the Church as the instrument he established for continuing to teach his dogmatic and moral truth, we must be discerning, but at the same time careful not to be numbered among the disagreeable children in

Jesus' comparison. Some people, forgetful that we're all members of Jesus' Mystical Body called the Church, have nothing good to say about clergymen, from the pope through cardinals and bishops down to priests and deacons.

There are many other practical consequences from Jesus' words. One is that our pulls in many directions can result in lukewarmness. This lack of fervor and state of ongoing half-heartedness pretends to justify itself with maxims like, "one shouldn't be petty"; "God is too big and magnanimous to bother about little things like this"; or "everybody's doing it." Lukewarmness is a gentle slope down which a person slips further and further from God. Almost without noticing, the person becomes content with staying just within the boundaries which separate him or her from complete carelessness. Where there's lukewarmness, there's no true worship of God at Mass, and prayer becomes vague, woolly, and distracted, with no real personal conversation with Our Lord.

We need joyful people who dance readily, and compassionate people who will always be quick to sympathize. We need those who are austere as well as those who are more easygoing and sociable. We need introvert perfectionists as well as extrovert dreamers. Jesus is pleading with us to give a person who's different from us a chance. We mustn't judge harshly or quickly condemn. As members of God's assembly and the human family, we must be anxious to profit from *all* the talents around us.

There are, God knows, roles for everyone. Little Jimmie was trying out for a part in a school play. He'd set his heart on being in it, though his mother feared he wouldn't be chosen. On the day the parts were awarded, with some trepidation his mother went to collect him after school. Jimmie rushed up to her, eyes shining with pride and excitement. "Guess what, Mom," he shouted, and said, "I've been chosen to clap and cheer!"

To follow Jesus' teachings is, as he intimates in his last words today, the way of wisdom. That's also the way of the message of solemn promise in today's reading from Isaiah. Echoing for those who obey God's word the same kind of victorious vindication as came to Abraham, our father in faith, Isaiah provides not only the spirit of a hymn of praise but also power and achievement to God's word. If we totally obey the divine word, our "prosperity will be like a river," and "vindication like the waves of the sea" will ensue.

Saturday, Second Week of Advent

Si 48:1-4, 9-11; Mt 17:10-13

Unity

The prophets, John the Baptist, and Jesus all shared in at least one thing: the hostility of their contemporaries to God's Good News. In a way that's applicable to all of us, coming close to God and allowing Him entry into our lives inevitably entails some suffering. Advent, which celebrates our anticipation of the coming of God, adds this note of suffering in order to be realistic about what discipleship entails. Human life, as the celebration of the Lord's birth shows, is shot through with a mixture of sadness and joy.

Jesus' words in today's gospel repeat what he had said at other times — namely, that whereas the scribes had taught one thing, he taught another. In this case, the scribes had said that the prophet Elijah would come back before the Messiah would arrive. That was because Elijah had been taken up from earth in a whirlwind (2 K 2:11 and in today's reading from Sirach) and the tradition arose that Elijah must return before "the great and terrible day" of the Lord (Ml 3:23). Jesus saw in John the Baptist the role of Elijah the persecuted prophet who was to usher in that day.

Today's passage from the Book of Sirach focuses on a single great accomplishment of Elijah: the re-establishment of *unity* within the tribes of Israel. We all recognize unity as *the* most difficult goal to achieve. Human nature propels people to try to get what they want despite any discord they cause. If a serious division sets in between members of a family, it seems impossible to restore love and agreement. When religious groups split from one another, we end up with staggering scandals like our current divisions within Christianity.

The birth of Jesus, like a newly born child in a home otherwise split, can be a force to bring about unity. Almost everybody loves babies. In the natural surrounding of the birth of the Christ-child at Christmas, God is suddenly appearing, as abruptly as did the prophet Elijah.

Because John the Baptist had confronted Herod Antipas the Tetrarch for his immoral union with his brother's wife, Herodias, he was beheaded. That scene was the opposite of the Advent values that we celebrate. Salome's dance was full of sexual innuendo and thoroughly demoralizing. It's easy to see through that besotted old lecher Herod Antipas who'd watched her, frozen, through a haze, looking like the ultimate tired businessman. "Wonderful," he said proprietarily at the dance's conclusion. But this voyeuristic episode took a lot out of him.

Herod Antipas was a soul encased in the jadedness that came from years of exercising ruthless power. His stomach strained against his shirt. He looked bleary and bloated and talked in the weary tones of a man who was long accustomed to people hanging on his every word. He was also, though, a man who could be betrayed into visible discomfort, at least momentarily, by his own appetites.

As for Salome, she was just beginning to appreciate the power she commanded over men. She spoke with the petulant breathiness of a movie starlet. When she danced, she succumbed to a gyrating, autoerotic frenzy that chilled even as it generated heat. The spectator had the feeling that perhaps he had no right to be watching.

Herodias had the grand carriage and stentorian tones of someone born to public life, streaked with a testy impatience with her less patrician husband. John the Baptist had a pale, wild-eyed visionary look and a voice that could peel flesh, both of which disturbed both Herodias and Herod Antipas.

Antipas on the one hand and Herodias and Salome on the other were different sides of the same coin. All were spoiled monsters, creatures of vast appetites used to getting what they wanted. Both Herod and Salome illustrate a dictum well known to people of power of all ages: Be careful what you wish for.

Because Jesus tried to bring dignity to people who were religious outlaws, he too began to be a victim of open persecution. Both the Baptist and Jesus stood for common decency, human dignity, and unity.

The unity which Jesus seeks expects us to form one family of love. Yet some of us at times continue to hold on to grudges, hurts, and bad memories. To continue with such division brings us ever closer to great tragedies like the beheading of John the Baptist and the crucifixion of Jesus.

As we enter further into the warmth and cheer of the Christmas season, we would be well advised to be more aware of our lack of unity with the suffering and poor in our midst who share so much of the cross and have so little of Christmas joy. May God grant us the strength to love *all* persons. May He give us also the grace to forgive and forget, so that we can bring about our finest gifts of charity to reunions in this season that are worthy of His Holy Spirit.

Monday, Third Week of Advent

Nb 24:2-7, 15-17; Mt 21:23-27

Commitment to Jesus' Authority

Some time ago (1960), a researcher conducted a famous social psychology experiment. It focused on the conflict between obedience to authority and personal conscience. In the experiment, a group of so-called "teachers" — actually the unknowing subjects of the experiment — were asked to administer an electric shock of increasing intensity to a "learner" for each mistake he made. The fictitious story given to the "teachers" was that the experiment was exploring effects of punishment for incorrect responses on learning behavior. The "teacher" wasn't aware that the "learners" were actually actors who were merely indicating more and more intense discomfort as the "teacher" increased the electric shocks which, unknown to the "teachers," were fake.

When the "teacher" asked the supervisor whether increased shocks should be given, he/she was verbally encouraged to continue. Sixty percent of the "teachers" obeyed orders to punish the learner to the very end of the 450-volt scale. None stopped before reaching 300 volts.

At times, the worried "teachers" questioned the experimenter, asking who was responsible for any harmful effects resulting from electric shocks at such a high level. Upon receiving the answer that the experimenter assumed full responsibility, teachers seemed to accept the response and continued shocking, even though some were extremely uncomfortable in doing so. Only about 40 percent of the "teachers" resisted and chose not to punish the "learners" even after being "absolved" of responsibility.

Like that experiment, today's gospel has to do with authority and responsibility. Jesus had just cleansed the Temple of its moneychangers. He had hit the leaders where it hurt them most:

in their pocketbooks (for they loved money). So now they tried to destroy his reputation.

The chief priests and elders who questioned Jesus about his authority constituted an official delegation of the Sanhedrin, the highest authority in the land: the legislative, executive, and judicial, all rolled into one. Jesus would have no authority to cleanse the Temple unless he were the Messiah. But it would be of no avail for him to tell them his identity outright, for he had already given them more than sufficient proof of his messiahship and they wouldn't accept it.

Jesus invited the chief priests and elders to open their hearts so that they might understand the truth of John the Baptist's ministry as well as his own. But they weren't interested in truth: they wanted *power*. Thus they missed the freedom that comes with accepting truth.

Jesus countered their question about his authority by asking about the divine or human origin of John the Baptist's baptism. It would be extremely difficult for the Jerusalem authorities to recognize John's baptism as divinely authorized and yet deny status to the man about whom John had preached and to whom John had humbly deferred. Their answer that they didn't know, although only a subterfuge, was an admission of failure in their official duty, for one of the chief functions of the Sanhedrin was to judge and condemn false prophets.

The Messiah and the prophets — in today's case, John the Baptist — are very often met by people who look for ways to avoid commitment. Commitment carries risks. The chief priests and elders had personal reasons for fearing commitment to anyone or anything outside themselves: fear of losing their authority and position. Many people in our society are afraid of any commitment beyond the next few minutes for similar reasons.

Our first readings this week all give passages from the Hebrew Scriptures which point to the coming of the Christ. In today's first reading, the foreign soothsayer Balaam had had an experience with God who confronted him on the road and brought him to the point of repentance for his rebellion.

Balaam was willing to speak only those words which God put into his mouth. King Balak of Moab sent representatives to this soothsayer, urging him to put a curse upon Israel. Balaam refused the first request; with God's permission, however, he accepted a second invitation, but was to do exactly what God would tell him.

On his journey, as a passage before today's tells us with a touch of humor, Balaam was toying with the hope that the Lord might eventually change the message to one congenial to the Moabite king. An angel of the Lord obstructed the road and the soothsayer's donkey refused to go forward. After it had been beaten three times, the donkey began to talk back to its owner. Balaam then saw the hitherto invisible angel and sensed the danger of refusing God's command. He promised to follow the instructions of God rather than be an instrument of King Balak.

Against the request of the Moabite king and against his own inclination, Balaam invoked a fourfold blessing over Israel. Today's reading contains Balaam's fourth such speech from God. In it he predicted the renowned star to advance from Jacob and the scepter of the king to rise from Israel. The "star" and the "scepter" were symbols of the monarchy. Balaam concluded with a prediction of the fate of various nations. This final prediction, though applicable in a limited sense to King David, was fulfilled by Jesus — the Christ, the Messiah — who established his kingdom upon the ruins of the empire of the pagan world. Jesus' Apostles sometimes derived useful lessons from the prophecy of Balaam (see, for example, 2 P 2:15f.).

Both of today's readings reach deeply into the flesh and blood of human life. The pagan prophet Balaam, despite his greedy desire for royal gifts, couldn't resist the compelling inspiration of the people whom God had led out of Egypt. John the Baptist preached the solid virtues of honesty, generosity, hope, humility, and loyalty.

Part of our preparation for the celebration of Jesus' birth is the renewal of our commitment to the authority of Jesus. The nature and depth of that commitment is a good subject for reflection.

Tuesday, Third Week of Advent

Zp 3:1f., 9-13; Mt 21:28-32

Personal Responsibility

Legend tells of a woman who wanted all sorts of good things for the world. One day, having decided to go shopping for some of them, she went into a mall and entered a store. She was surprised to see Jesus behind the counter. She knew it was Jesus, because he looked just like the devotional pictures she'd seen. She looked again and again at him, and finally got up her nerve to ask, "Excuse me, are you Jesus?" "I am." "Do you work here?" "No, I own the store." "Oh, what do you sell in here?" "Oh, just about anything!" "Anything?" "Yes, anything you want. What do you want?" She said, "I don't know." "Well," Jesus said, "feel free to walk up and down the aisles, see what you want, make a list, and then come back and we'll see what we can do for you."

She did just that. She picked things like peace on earth, the eradication of hunger and poverty, the elimination of drugs, harmony among people, good families, clean air, and the careful use of resources. In fact, by the time she got back to the counter, she had a long list. Jesus took the list, skimmed it, looked up at her and smiled, "No problem." Then he bent down behind the counter and picked out all sorts of packets, stood up, and laid them on the counter. She asked, "What are these?" Jesus replied, "Seed packets." She said, "You mean I don't get the finished product?" "No, you come and see what your dreams look like, and I give you the seeds. You go home and plant the seeds, nurture them, and help them to grow; usually someone else reaps the benefits." "Oh," she said — and left the store without buying anything.

Her rejection of personal responsibility would undoubtedly be supported by current allegations in some quarters that it's genes that cause behavior, taking away personal responsibility. That "genocentric" view turns personal responsibility into genetic destiny: "I'm not guilty, Your Honor, my genes made me do it."

In today's gospel, Jesus wants to show that, because of the way each group addresses personal responsibility, sinners are making their way to the kingdom of God while many so-called "religious" people are not. He gave a simple example of a man with two sons. The elder son, who represents the Pharisees, put on a pious appearance and always said and did the right thing, or at least made people think that he did. He conned his father by agreeing to work in the vineyard — and didn't. His response was pious, deferential — and insincere.

The other son was mischievous, disobedient, saucy, and self-willed. He replied first with a quick "No" to work in the vineyard before he had time to think. But then he went out and worked in the vineyard. He was like the tax collectors and prostitutes, the male and female occupations considered to be the most shameful in Palestine then.

These people quietly changed their life and humbly returned to God, determined to "do no wrong and speak no lies," as the prophet Zephaniah had advised. Lying for some people gives an ecstasy of freedom: they become unknowable, unaccountable at the moments they lie. Some people are so in the habit of lying that they lie even when truth would serve them better.

In the days of Zephaniah, all Israel was reduced to a condition of never allowing tax collectors and prostitutes to forget what they were. In today's passage, the prophet cried out about that. Zephaniah uttered a warning about those who took no rebuke to heart and continued in their wrong-doing. He included a vision of hope: God will bring a faithful remnant of His people back to the dignity of their first creation. Both sons in Jesus' story were imperfect. Even the son who did the work after regretting his refusal spoiled his doing good by the ungracious way he did it. Yet it's far more noble to change your mind and do good than to remain set in the direction of evil. The ideal way is, of course, both to promise and to do, and that with graciousness. Jesus points to John the Baptist as a model: he had lived an austerely holy life and died for it.

Ever since Adam blamed Eve and Eve blamed the serpent, it seems part of human nature to want to "pass the buck." But for the responsibility of the making of our lives, the buck stops with each of us. As we prepare to celebrate the birth of the Son of God, it's appropriate that we look at the nature of our "yes" to God in baptism. Prayer, public profession of faith, regular sharing in the Church's public worship, all look like a "yes" to God; how we act toward the poor and unloved in our midst, and to family members and friends who have a special claim on us, determines whether, after having said "yes," we actually go to work in the Lord's vineyard.

A specific example of what we can shop for is the Christmas angel's message of "peace on earth." Since the first century of Our Lord, almost 149 million people have died in major wars around the world. Currently, the United States spends trillions of dollars on nuclear weapons every few years. The entire face of the earth would be different if that vast sum had been employed on development. Famine, illiteracy, and disease would not be the daily companion of some of the 3.5 billion people (out of a total of close to 7 billion) who live in degrading conditions unworthy of the human family.

Are we in our daily lives like either of the two sons in Jesus' story? Of course, taking stock of one's soul, regularly and systematically, isn't encouraged by a culture that makes "I'm learning not to be hard on myself" a guiding principle. We might well imitate Judaism's "Al Khet" prayer, which is a collective confession of sins, literally an alphabetical listing of everything from arrogance to violence and beyond. The range is staggering — of sins you've committed, sins you'd never think of doing, and sins that sound so exciting you wish you'd committed them.

There are always warnings against simply changing one's conduct without changing one's heart. Concentrating on our underlying dispositions, are we able to learn by our mistakes and have a change of heart? As we prepare for Christmas, it's helpful to remember our personal responsibility for our life. To be or not to be — the doubts and questions of a Hamlet are those of all of us to some degree: to do or not to do, to commit ourselves or not to commit ourselves, to accept responsibility or not to accept it.

Wednesday, Third Week of Advent

Is 45:6-8, 18, 21-25; Lk 7:18-23

Both Light and Darkness Are from God

According to the Jewish historian Josephus, John the Baptist had been imprisoned by Herod in the frontier fortress of Machaerus, situated on a high plateau to the east of the Dead Sea. It was from the loneliness and barbarity of that place that John sent his disciples to ask Jesus if he were "the one who is to come" — one of the regular titles of the Messiah.

Did John the Baptist ask this question of Jesus for the sake of his disciples? They were, after all, somewhat scandalized by Jesus' less rigorous rules on fasting and other of John's practices, and envious of Jesus' success; perhaps they also shared the common people's ideas of a militant Messiah. Discussions on the Messiah must have been more vehement among John's disciples than the rest of the people, because they had been more intensely interested in the works of God.

Or did John send his question to Jesus for his own sake? John had, after all, expected a strong Messiah — if we go by his preaching, a Messiah to come with fire and whirlwind. Jesus' gentle mercy didn't fit that picture. If the question was to help John himself, what agonizing hours must have been behind that question! Even a prophet's life is shaken by storms and saddled with weaknesses. At times the Holy Spirit hoists John the Baptist far above the heights of human accomplishment; at other times, the Spirit plunges him headlong into darkness. (A moving and powerful picture of the essence and destiny of the prophetic life is in 1 Kings 17 and 19.)

Jesus couldn't answer the question directly by saying, "Yes, I am the Messiah," because the people had a wrong idea of who the Messiah was supposed to be, and the Pharisees would interpret that answer as blasphemy. At the same time he couldn't answer, "No, I'm not," because that would be a lie. So he drew John's disciples' attention to the miracles he was working: healing the blind, the lame, the deaf, the lepers.

Jesus was pointing out how these miracles fulfilled the Messianic prophecies given throughout the Book of Isaiah (cf. Is 29:18ff.; 35:5f.; 61:1). Everyone would recognize Isaiah's words even though Jesus didn't mention the prophet's name. According to Isaiah in today's first reading, the Lord creates both light and darkness — well-being and misery. Jesus' burst of sunlight assured that he is the promised one.

Yet the working of miracles isn't sufficient proof of the Messiah — prophets had worked them, and Elijah and Elisha had even raised the dead. Above and beyond all that, though, in a time that had no high regard for ordinary people Jesus reminded them that the poor were having the Good News preached to them. He concluded his answer by asserting a beatitude: that the one who takes no offense at him is blessed.

Today's scriptures place clearly before us the biblical expectation of faith: Jesus is the Lord of both life and death, of both light and darkness, of both strength and weakness. We can be swept away by joy and prosperity and totally *forget* the presence of God; we can be embittered by pain and disappointment and *rebel* against God. No amount of reasoning can explain why God creates and directs darkness and misery as much as He forms light and well-being.

John the Baptist, like many saints, lived much of his life in spiritual darkness. The darkness can be our friend as well as the light. It's only in the darkness that we can see the splendor of the universe — blankets of stars, the solitary glow of distant planets. It was darkness that allowed the Magi to find the star that guided them to where the Christ-child lay. In the darkness of night, desert peoples find relief from the cruel relentless heat of the sun; in the blessed desert darkness Mary and Joseph were able to flee with the infant Jesus to safety in Egypt. In the darkness of the womb, we've all been nurtured and protected. In the darkness of sleep, we're soothed, restored, and renewed.

In the solitude of darkness, we sometimes remember those who need God's presence in a special way — the sick, the unemployed, the bereaved, the persecuted, the homeless; those who are demoralized and discouraged, those whose fear has turned to cynicism, those whose insecurity has become bitterness. Sometimes in the darkness, we remember those who are near to our hearts — colleagues, partners, parents, children, neighbors, friends.

Sometimes in the solitude of darkness, our fears and concerns, our hopes and our visions, magnify. We come face to face with ourselves and with the road that lies ahead of us. And in that darkness, we find companionship for the journey. In that same darkness, we sometimes allow ourselves to wonder and worry whether the human race is going to survive.

In the darkness that contains both our hopelessness and our expectancy, we watch for a sign of God's hope. We know that God is with us, and yet we still await His coming. We go forth as preparers and proclaimers of Jesus, a light far off that nothing will put out. In the darkness, God gives us sufficient signs to discover Him.

But we need good interior dispositions. Among those dispositions are sincerity, humility, a clean heart, a sense of the presence of God, and an outlook that interprets and judges events from the perspective of faith. We need a turning toward God before Christmas, so as to contemplate Him with a clearer look when we come to celebrate His revelation of His humanity.

Thursday, Third Week of Advent

Is 54:1-10; Lk 7:24-30

Smiling for Christmas

Some people say that flattery will get you nowhere, but that's not always true. The business of advertising constitutes a vast industry devoted to puffery, which is a form of flattery, and brings in big profits.

For the most part, flattery is harmless. Surrounding the flattered with a halo of good feeling, it gives away nothing really worth having, but it may get a lot in return. Through flattery I confirm your self-love, so that you're well disposed toward me. We've all learned to nod and smile and hold our tongue and murmur approval. As Casanova taught, you always tell beauty that it's intelligent, and intelligence that it's beautiful.

In today's gospel, Jesus praises John the Baptist lest the people conclude from the question of John's disciples about Jesus' Messiahship that John himself had lost faith in Jesus. Jesus waits till John's messengers are leaving, however, lest he seem to be currying the Baptist's favor by flattering John before his disciples.

As we saw yesterday, it was just before this that John — in jail for bluntly condemning Herod Antipas for his defiant adultery with his brother's wife — had sent his disciples to searchingly inquire of Jesus whether he was "He Who Is To Come" — the Messiah, the long-expected savior of the Jewish people — or whether they had to wait for someone else.

Jesus had resorted to quoting the prophet Isaiah, knowing that the intelligent among the people would realize that he was answering "Yes, I am the Messiah," but in an astute way that would give the leaders a hard time if they tried to pin him down in court. (See Lk 7:18-23, yesterday's reading.)

Jesus went on to establish the full identity of John as a prophet — that he was a person who spoke on God's behalf. Despite John's emaciated frame, rags, and imprisonment, Jesus gave him great praise. Jesus knew full well that everybody recognized that John's blunt, courageous character was anything but weak. Therefore, he asked the people why they took the trouble to leave the comfort of the city to go out into the disagreeable desert to see John. Did they think that John was comparable to a reed swaying in the wind (v. 24) — a weak thing that wavers? Or did they expect to see a man dressed in luxury (v. 25)? Everyone knew that one of John's characteristics was his rough garments. Jesus' questions were a neat reference against Herod Antipas.

Jesus called John something even more than a prophet (v. 26) because, while the Jewish prophets pointed out the Messiah at a distance, John in his prophetic office pointed him out directly, physically, and close-up.

Despite that testimony to John's greatness, though, Jesus said that the least born into the kingdom of God is greater than John. Why? Because John, great though he was, understood only half of the identity of God as shown through Jesus. John lived before the cross, so he could never know the full extent of God's love. The New Dispensation, in which every disciple of Christ is mystically united with the Son of God, is so far superior to the Old that even the least in the kingdom of heaven is greater than anyone before it.

From today's biblical readings we realize that God's "Advent" comes in several ways. It may involve a long preparation, the way of Isaiah's centuries-old traditions. Or it can be more immediate, as with John the Baptist. Or it may be our current Advent season for us.

In our preparing for the coming of the Lord, we may at times think that we have to be contortionists to get along. We've got to keep our back against the wall, our ear to the ground, our shoulder to the wheel, our nose to the grindstone, and at the same time keep a level head and both feet on the ground. And we're supposed to have our head in the clouds so we can look for the silver lining.

Through it all, it's appropriate that we smile. A medical condition called Moebius Syndrome causes babies to be born unable to smile. They don't have all the muscles in their face. Along with not being able to close their mouth and eyes all the way, they don't have clear speech. With no movement in their face, they aren't able to show emotion through facial expression.

The parents of one child born with this condition — Becky Peterson — searched high and low for a doctor who did the kind of surgery that Becky needed. When she was 16, she had the first of 20 major surgeries to enable her to smile. In the end, the surgery was successful, and Becky smiled wherever she went.

It remained her greatest joy to greet everyone she saw with a smile and a "hello." Smiling at people she didn't know, she figured that that might be the only time in their day that someone might take the time to be nice to them. Having thought about it, she concluded that if everyone would just be kind to others, smile at them, and treat them the way they would want to be treated, the world would be a much more peaceful place. It broke Becky's heart to see how some people take smiling for granted. She thanked God every day for putting a smile on her face, and wished that everyone in the world would realize what a precious gift a smile is and use it more often and more sincerely.

May the Lord enable us this Advent to prepare for His coming by a deeper attitude of both faith and joy — and a smile!

Friday, Third Week of Advent

Is 56:1-3, 6-8; Jn 5:33-36

Tear Down Walls

According to the Law of Moses, people couldn't bear witness in their own behalf. Jesus asserts that four witnesses bear testimony to him. First (v. 33) he mentions John the Baptist. Second (v. 36) are the works that he has been performing. Third is the heavenly Father who sent him. Lastly, in a line shortly after our gospel today (v. 39), are the Sacred Scriptures. We've already seen in our Advent readings something of the witness of John the Baptist, Jesus' works, and his heavenly Father. That leaves us to consider some of the witness of the Sacred Scriptures to Jesus.

Part of the scriptural testimony to Jesus is today's first reading, written six centuries before Christ by the disciples of Isaiah. At that time some of the Jews' original enthusiasm over their return from Exile had begun to wane. In addition to the literal walls of their Temple to keep people out, they were putting up metaphorical walls to do the same. Isaiah contradicted all that. He extended a welcome, calling God's house "a house of prayer for all peoples" (v. 7), an expression that Jesus would quote when he cleansed the Temple of moneychangers.

In today's world, in which the tables are turned, walls are built to keep Jews out, and anti-Judaism rears its head, it's good to remind ourselves of some things. Jesus was a Jew. He was born under the Law (Torah), presented in the Temple, circumcised, made a pilgrimage to the Temple at age twelve, and was so expert in the teachings of the Law of Moses that his Apostles (and at times even his enemies) often called him "rabbi."

He based his central commandment of love on an amended teaching of the Jewish Scriptures. As his Apostles he chose twelve Jews, symbolizing the twelve tribes of Israel, upon whom he set up his Church. In his last days on earth he observed the Passover supper, and on the cross he recited a Psalm of David. He was buried according to Jewish custom. After his death and Resurrection and the coming of the Holy Spirit, the Apostles continued for years to worship in synagogues and observe Jewish law.

Uprooted from its native soil, however, the Church became de-Judaized, and anti-Jewish sentiments developed. Some Christian misunderstandings revolved around the idea that the Jews as a people and all their descendants bore collective guilt for the death of Jesus.

As "proof" of this charge of "deicide" people hostile to Jews would take various phrases from different gospels and put them together to tell a story that none of the four Evangelists would have recognized as true. For instance, the cry for Jesus' blood to be "on us and on our children" is recounted only in the gospel of St. Matthew (27:25), where it's the cry of only a small group of people in Pilate's courtyard. If, however, you take from the gospel of St. John the expression "the Jews" or "the Judeans" — a generalization used only in John the Evangelist — and attach it to Matthew's text as if all the Jews cried that Jesus' blood be upon them, you have an implication of collective guilt found only in the textual manipulation.

Around such misunderstandings of the gospels arose over the centuries what has been called a "teaching of contempt" against Jews and Judaism: for instance, the idea that as divine punishment the Jews suffered the destruction of the Jerusalem Temple, are cursed by God for their crime, and are condemned to perpetual wandering. In the Christian Middle Ages, Jews were often humiliated, ghettoized, harassed, and even murdered.

On the other hand, the *Catechism of the Council of Trent* in the sixteenth century argued that "our sins made the Lord Christ suffer" and "our crime in this case is greater in us than in the Jews," since what the involved Jews of Jesus' time did was done in ignorance. "We [Christians], however, profess to know him, and when we deny him by our deeds, we seem in some way to lay violent hands on him" (*Roman Catechism* 1, 5, 11).

The Second Vatican Council in 1965 restated this tenet of our faith, writing that one can't blame all the Jews of Jesus' time "nor Jews today" for Jesus' death, and adding that "the Jews must not be spoken of as rejected by God or accursed." It did this particularly by recalling the positive implications of the text of St. Paul's Letter to the Romans (9-11), which says that to the Jews belong "the covenants and the promises."

A very early consequence of the Vatican II position was that the Church's sole official prayer for the Jewish people, the Good Friday prayer, was rewritten. Whereas for centuries that prayer had been for the conversion of Jews to Christianity, now it asks God to strengthen Jews in their already faithful response to God's call to them and to bring them to the "fullness of redemption" at the end of time. Also, Pope John Paul II not only visited the Great Synagogue of Rome for the first time in the two-millennia history of Jewish-Christian relations, but prayed there with them in praise of the One God of Israel. And he made a pilgrimage to Jerusalem, inserting into the Western Wall, like millions of pious Jews, a prayer; his prayer explicitly begged God's forgiveness for the sins of Christians against Jews over the centuries.

We need new theological language in this area. Where, for one, do we categorize Judaism, which the *Catechism of the Catholic Church* describes as "unlike other world religions" because it's "already a response to God's revelation in the Old Covenant," a revelation neither relativized nor replaced by God's revelation to humankind in Christ? Where do the Jews fit in the Church's mission to the Gentiles? Another major issue that will be with us for some time is coming to terms with our mutual historical memories of the Holocaust (*Shoah*) and of events in the centuries preceding it.

Since the Nazi atrocities, most mainline churches have issued documents (like the Roman Catholic *Nostra Aetate*) which have in one way or another condemned anti-Judaism as un-Christian, called for a cessation of teaching that depicts Jews as rejects of God, emphasized the rich Jewish roots of Christianity, affirmed the validity and permanence of God's covenant with the Jewish people, and called for fraternal dialogue between Christians and Jews for at least the minimal level of promoting cooperation in the pursuit of social justice, peace, and other common goals. Both sides are urged to what the Jews call *teshuva* and Christians call repentance.

Realizing that all of us set up walls which separate us from God and from one another, let's try to develop an attitude of humility and the avoidance of arrogance or smugness that can turn other people away from what we stand for. And let's develop compassion, by which we can truly "feel with" the sufferings of others to the point of making the walls that separate the human family come tumbling down.

That would truly make the kind of world that the first Christmas was intended to bring.

December 17

Gn 49:2, 8-10; Mt 1:1-17

Jesus' Family Tree

Today, many people are interested in their family tree. They may want to learn something about themselves, or — especially these days of awareness of DNA — perhaps find some of their health inheritance from an ancestor. In today's gospel, St. Matthew presents the family tree of Jesus because, for one, among the Jews as among other peoples of nomadic origin, the genealogical tree was of capital importance. Persons were known fundamentally by the clan or tribe to which they belonged rather than by the place where they lived.

Matthew rejoices in telling us in the very first line of his gospel that Jesus Christ is "the son of David." That's similar to St. Luke's gospel (2:4), which tells us that Jesus "was descended from the house and family of David." Matthew wanted to show his fellow Jews for whom he intended his gospel that Jesus was in the line from which the prophets had foretold the Messiah would come. Jesus was registered in the royal house through St. Joseph, since, as St. Ambrose said, he who came into the world ought to be registered according to the custom of the world.

David was extremely important, to the history of Israel as well as the history of our Savior. Yet that importance is also mysterious. It's a bit startling to hear the liturgy rejoicing in David's family heritage, because when you look at David's *family* realities rather than at the military and political realities in which he excelled, there could hardly be a greater inheritance of trouble than being born into "the house and family of David."

In many ways, David was a magnificent man: generous, loyal, affectionate, gifted, and full of life. He was a comradely freedom fighter, an ardent religious believer, and a dedicated if increasingly confused king. His kingdom was a high point in Jewish history. Modern Judaism looks to him with great favor, and the Israeli flag is centered around the Star of David (*mogen David*). That star has become a general sign of Judaism.

But David was a shatteringly unsuccessful father. Inasmuch as he had about seventeen sons (2 S 3:2-5, etc.), his lack of fatherly prudence was magnified. It's not that he didn't care. Far from being a cold father, David seems to have been overly indulgent with his grown-up sons. "My son Absalom! My son, my son Absalom! If only I had died instead of you, Absalom, my son, my son!" (2 S 19:1) — that famous lament of David was over a traitor-son who had schemed against him, lied to him, and then died fighting him for the throne.

In a similar vein, the story of Amnon (2 S 13), David's firstborn who entrapped his half-sister Tamar, raped her, and threw her out into a ruined future, is a chronicle of a spoiled child. David's inexcusable response when he heard of the rape was to become angry, but he wouldn't punish his son.

What a change from David's original condition! When we first meet David (1 S 16), he's a model son in a hardworking sheep-ranching family in the rough hills of Judea. He's spirited, but he's also obedient, disciplined, and profoundly responsive to urgent adult concerns.

How did David arrive at his failures as a father a few decades later? The story seems, for one thing, a classic study of the results of social change. Such changing times are always hard, especially on parents. When the rules of society are changing, in the confusion it becomes harder to persuade rambunctious young people to act in an orderly, civilized way.

But David's transition involved more than social change. In the generation before David came of age, the people had chosen to have a king (1 S 8:5) and thus be "like the other nations." Their first king was Saul. Kings were expected to be magnificent, so gross economic inequality was taken for granted. Kings, in the only models then available, had harems, not only to express sexual prowess but also to forge political alliances.

Each of David's seventeen princelings from several wives was thought to need his own mule (their equivalent of an expensive convertible) and his own retinue. David himself hadn't been brought up like that. But the novelty of a "court" seems to have dazzled him. Far from teaching his children responsibility and discipline, he let them live a luxurious life. His family life disintegrated into turmoil, scheming, distrust, and contradictory ambitions. David himself became a wheeler-dealer, endlessly duplicitous, and weak enough to have sinned greatly.

One of his sins was adultery. David, in his leisure, spotted the beautiful Bathsheba bathing on her roof. In his passion, he quickly seduced her. The scriptures describing the occasion (2 S 12) give no indication of conversation, caring, affection, or love. At the end of the encounter, Bathsheba was only "the woman." Her first reported words came later, and they were devastating: "I'm pregnant."

The swift plot became deadly when David furloughed Uriah, Bathsheba's army husband, and tried to wheedle him into her bed so David's paternity would be unknown. When that plan failed, David took his cover-up a desperate step further: He made sure that Uriah was killed in battle. Then he married Bathsheba. From that union, King Solomon was born.

That sin cut so deeply into the life of David and ancient Israel that it rivals in power the sin of Adam and Eve. Yet because of his repentance David was forgiven. His Psalm 50 is the voice of a man who realizes that he's profoundly alienated from God and has come to the point of comprehending that he simply can't go on that way.

Everyone took for granted that God's promises to David (2 S 7) meant what they said: that an offspring of the Davidic line would be enthroned as king of Judah and Israel. And when the dynasty was humiliated or even deprived of all royal privileges, the people could only question and remonstrate with God and ask (in the words of Psalm 89), "How long will it be?"

Another humbling observation about Jesus' human ancestry is that it mentions, in addition to Bathsheba, three other women: Tamar, Rahab, and Ruth. Tamar had dressed as a temple prostitute to win Judah's favor and conceive a child through him (Gn 38). Rahab, a harlot of Jericho, helped two of Joshua's spies escape from Jericho (Jos 2); yet the New Testament mentions her faith (Heb 11:31) and good works (Jm 2:25). Ruth, who entered biblical history as a polytheist, came to the bed of Boaz at night to inveigle him into marrying her (Rt 3). Bathsheba was the wife of a gentile — a Hittite; Tamar and Rahab were Canaanites, and Ruth was a Moabite.

The last woman to be named is Mary, who acquired royal privileges through her husband Joseph. The irregular unions in Jesus' family tree were strange foreshadowings of the virginal conception of Jesus by Mary.

Today's readings allow several conclusions. First, by his family tree Matthew shows that Jesus is fully human. He's like us in everything but sin (as the Letter to the Hebrews tells us). He shares all the emotional, physical, and psychological burdens — as well as the joys — of being human, to show us that he understands what we go through.

Secondly, we're perhaps surprised to see how God exercised

great patience and understanding throughout the highs and lows in the history of Israel in preparing a people to become the people of the Messiah. God continually allows the great gift of freedom in our personal history, too.

Lastly, Advent is very much about how we welcome the Lord. The season of Advent urges us to open ourselves wide by frequent, genuine, from-the-heart prayer, to make so much space within ourselves that the Lord is able to fill us with his presence.

December 18

Jr 23:5-8; Mt 1:18-24

St. Joseph, Model of Advent

Today's portion of St. Matthew's gospel is a demonstration of the truth of G.K. Chesterton's wise and humorous statement that whoever tries to fit God into their minds ends up with a cracked skull. After his genealogy of Jesus (which we contemplated yesterday) Matthew comes to the engagement of Joseph and Mary (v. 18). For the Jews at that time, marriage took place in three stages: simple engagement; betrothal or espousal, which in Galilee usually lasted a year; and marriage proper. Here Matthew refers to the second stage, during which unfaithfulness was considered as adultery and was punishable by death.

St. Joseph, like Mary, often had to ponder. Pondering in the gospels doesn't mean what it meant for the Greek philosophers like Socrates, Plato, and Aristotle. For them, to ponder meant to take seriously Socrates' dictum that the unexamined life isn't worth living.

In the gospels, however, which exhibit more the Hebrew

way of understanding life, to ponder is less a question of intellectually contemplating something as it is of patiently holding a mystery inside of one's soul, complete with all the tension that brings. When Joseph went over and over his situation, he was pondering in the biblical sense. He was standing before one of life's great mysteries carrying an indescribable tension that he was helpless to resolve and must simply live with. Joseph, newly engaged to Mary, couldn't accept the blatant implication that Mary had been unfaithful to him, but he couldn't deny the fact that Mary was pregnant.

On the one side Joseph was a righteous man. He wanted to observe the Mosaic Law. That Law entitled him, at the very least, to repudiate his marriage agreement by signing a declaration to that effect in the presence of witnesses, but without having to state his reasons in public. The Law gave him also the right on the other hand to renounce Mary publicly, in which case her punishment would be death.

If Joseph did nothing, there could be other bad consequences. For one thing, it wouldn't be honorable for him to assume the paternity of a child whom he knew wasn't his, especially in view of the Mosaic Law's requirements of justice. Besides, should he fail to denounce Mary, his failure, if the true paternity came to light, might be taken as evidence of a disgraceful connivance on his part in her sin.

Because Joseph never wanted to do anything unkind, he decided to quietly divorce Mary and disappear from a mystery beyond his comprehension. But when his sincerity reached its limit, there came a further mystery. A message from God told him not to be afraid to take Mary as his wife. The message said that it was through the Holy Spirit that this child had been conceived (v. 20).

At first, it must have seemed to him, as it had to the prophet Jeremiah, that the Lord's pronouncements were being annulled and profaned, not sanctified and accomplished. Jeremiah, like

Isaiah, had witnessed the deterioration of the Davidic dynasty. Kings who succeeded to David's throne were apostates like Ahaz or weaklings like Zedekiah. Even if God were to be faithful to His assurances to David of an everlasting dynasty, it was a disservice to support a corrupt royal house.

In Joseph's case, the angel's message went on to direct that he take the responsibility of naming the child "Jesus," a name that means "savior" because, as the message said, "he will save his people from their sins" (v. 21).

To the mystified Joseph, one thing was sure: God was making it abundantly clear that the child being discussed was special. After arriving at a conclusion which cost him excruciatingly agonizing soul-searching, Joseph followed the angel's advice and accepted Mary as his wife.

Matthew saw significance in the name given by the prophet Isaiah — "Emmanuel": "God is with us," which means that the Lord is with His people. Matthew considered this appellation so important that the very last sentence of his gospel would have the departing Jesus say "I am with you always" (28:20). What does it really mean for God to be "with us"? He's with us in coming to live among us (the Word was made flesh, and dwelt among us). He's with us in being on our side against our spiritual foes (If God is with us, who can be against us?). He's with us in that he understands us (he knows, from the inside, our deepest anxieties).

We, like Joseph, can be faced with puzzling and agonizing situations which seem to deny God's goodness and justice. Not the least of Joseph's virtues was that he didn't work for mere appearances and neglect what is solid and within. His virtues were interior, practiced away from public view, and under the eye of God alone. He sought God in simplicity, found God in detachment, and enjoyed God's company in obscurity.

Joseph loved Mary with such generosity of heart that, when he learned of her desire to preserve the consecration she had made to God, he nonetheless agreed to marry her. He would rather renounce having children than live apart from the woman he loved. His was a pure, refined, and deep love, full of respect with no hint of selfishness.

Let's go to Joseph, so that he may teach us to live side by side with Jesus and Mary. Joseph, full of admiration, unspeaking and respectful, contemplates the child and his mother. After Mary, he was the first person to see the Son of God made man. No one could have experienced more happiness than he when he took in his arms the Messiah, who in no visible way could be distinguished from any other child.

Joseph saw the shepherds approach the cave, timid and curious, to see the baby wrapped in swaddling clothes. He heard them explain about the appearance of the heavenly messengers. Joseph contemplated the radiant happiness of the woman who was his wife, this marvelous lady who had been entrusted into his keeping. Enthralled by the way she gazed at her son, he saw her unspeakable joy, her overflowing love, her every gesture so full of exquisite tenderness. Joseph grasped the fact that his whole reason for being was this child, precisely because the child needed help and protection.

Are we willing to reflect, ponder, and struggle, as Joseph did, in discerning God's will in our lives? Like Joseph, we're to give God what's right — not what's left. And we're not to put a question mark in our lives where God puts a period or an exclamation point.

December 19

Jg 13:2-7, 24-25; Lk 1:2-25

Hope and Trust in God

It's a necessary part of our happiness to expect and hope for good things. Consider how we look forward to a break from the routine of daily work, how we anticipate getting away from miserable weather, how we live for the weekend. In some senses we *must* live in hope. Advent is a season of hope; in it we show our hope that all the best that we can wish for can come to us in Christ. The texts surrounding the Advent of the Lord are filled primarily with hope and assurances about what's to come.

Today's readings tell stories of women who had no hope of bearing a child. Samson's mother is one of several barren women in the Bible who were given children through a special act of God's mercy. Among others are Hannah the mother of Samuel, and Sarah the mother of Isaac; and, in today's reading from the New Testament, Elizabeth the mother of John the Baptist. Their children were all given for a special vocation. It's worth reflecting that all children are a precious gift from God, and all without exception have a vocation to love and serve Him in some unique way.

These barren couples, having accepted the situation, had arranged all the details of their married lives accordingly. Their home and income, their work and relaxation, their mental attitudes, their conversations, and everything about their relationships had been adjusted to their sad barrenness. Each woman was visited by an angel and given the message that, contrary to all expectations, she would have a son. How difficult it must be to revive hopes for having a child — to hope not to be let down again.

St. Luke's gospel reading today begins in the House of God with the angel announcing to Zechariah that his aged wife Elizabeth will conceive a son. Angels have cropped up in nearly every religion since time began. The Greeks had *lasas*, graceful female household spirits; the Jews saw angels everywhere; the Muslims have their own version; and angels hovered over the major events of Christianity.

We might think we'd like to be visited by an angel, but it's likely that most of us would prefer an angel in disguise. Real angels aren't chubby little babies or androgynous creatures in long white dresses who drift to earth on gossamer wings. Why we've pictured angels as delicate or tiny is a puzzlement, since the angels described in scripture are a lot more like heavenly Marine commandos — take-charge, no-nonsense beings carrying out divine orders.

The angels posted at the gates of Eden, for example, were armed with flaming swords. The angels described in the Book of Ezekiel — with their four faces, four wings, hooves of brass, and four hands — could have come straight from a science-fiction movie. The angel who appeared to Balaam, the pagan prophet, terrified Balaam's donkey into immobility. The angels singing over Bethlehem scared the poor shepherds witless.

It would take four centuries' distance from paganism before a Christian dared put wings on angels. (The wings signal omnipotence.) What's really terrifying is the chance that, because angels don't look as sweet, or as mundane, or as mysterious as we think they should, we won't recognize them. We may spend our whole lives entertaining angels unawares.

To Zechariah, the father-to-be of John the Baptist, the angel appeared within the gold-plated walls of the Temple at Jerusalem. To Mary six months later, he would appear in a humble home in Nazareth. The angel's appearance to Zechariah involved a large crowd; his appearance to Mary would be private. The encounter between the angel Gabriel and Zechariah was strained; the announcement to Mary would be tranquil. Though the angel had come to Zechariah without first addressing any greeting, because of the importance of the event the angel would greet Mary in highly complimentary terms. (Mary, more than any other human being in the Bible, was the recipient of the most impressive salutations [Lk 1:28, 30, 35, 42-45; 2:34].)

Whereas Zechariah had been fearful at seeing the angel, Mary would be greatly troubled — not in fear at the sight of the angel, but in amazement at the high-sounding titles. She wouldn't understand the full meaning of the message any more than Zechariah did; so she pondered — suggesting intense, prolonged reflection in a spirit of faith.

Zechariah had difficulty in believing that what was not humanly possible would happen. His response shows him half open to it and half closed: his faith in God's power went only so far. He could accept that one could experience God in a holy place like the Temple — but hardly in family life. This may explain the angel's rebuke that Zechariah would be mute until the birth of his son; it was a sign that God seeks to work in saving ways in and through the everyday exchanges in family and community.

Many of us don't know what it's like to struggle with barrenness as did Elizabeth and the other women in the scriptures. Even when the situation seems hopeless, we must never forsake hope but continue along our day-by-day line of duties, confident in God. We may have felt spiritually barren at times — stuck in proneness to sin, or sensing emptiness, or feeling too old to change our bad habits. Today's readings tell us that God can bring new life from barrenness.

In a spirit that's appropriate to these days that are close to Christmas, let's pray for an increase of hope and trust: trust in God because of all He has done for us through the coming of our Savior; trust to believe when things happen that we don't understand; trust in the Holy Spirit to enable us to recognize God at work in all the ordinary situations of joy and of sorrow in our lives.

December 20

Is 7:10-14; Lk 1:26-38

Mary, a Prelude to Christmas

To go and see the baby in the Christmas crèche is the simplest prayer in the world: Anyone can do it. We can wander in, gaze, comment, share our thoughts like the shepherds and Magi. Or we can simply look — the prayer of "simple regard." We can do this on our feet, like the shepherds; on our knees, like the Magi; or sitting, like mother Mary. Mary's face has the look of a girl both vulnerable and honored, flushed with incredulous joy, as though she's hearing or saying, "You're beautiful and I love you."

In front of her newborn baby, she adds to the wonder of contemplating the Christ-child all the power of her prayer before the angel Gabriel: "Here I am, the Lord's servant. Let it be done to me according to your word." It may be that Mary taught this prayer to her son, for he later prayed and taught others to pray that his heavenly Father's will be done.

As she sits and looks down at the baby, she's contemplating, as per Gabriel's promise, the Son of God (Lk 1:35). The title he would later choose for himself was "Son of Humanity." The words, originally from the Book of Daniel, are usually translated "Son of Man" but, with the development of language, that has become a less precise translation. By the title "Son of Humanity," Jesus put Mary in the position of representing all people, so that we're invited to identify with her: pray with her, rejoice with her, suffer with her, give thanks with her.

Contrary to the plaster-cast piety that often imprisons Mary, she's a person whom today's people, both men and women, can admire and imitate. As part of our prelude to Christmas, we pay honor to her who was to be the first dwelling-place of the Word Incarnate. At the time of God's announcement to Mary, her betrothal to Joseph entailed a commitment but no sexual privileges. At that time and place, betrothal occurred at the age of about twelve-and-a-half years and the couple usually married about a year later.

The essence of God's announcement to Mary had been that she would conceive and bear a son. Her wonder and awe at possibilities not consciously grasped prompted her direct question about how all this could possibly be, because she had no intimate relationship with any man. Respect for virginity had no parallel in pagan cults, and perhaps far too many young women today consider virginity as a form of immaturity that has to be discarded like losing baby teeth, or as a failure of courage. As a virtue, today experience has displaced innocence (which doesn't seem to have left women notably happier than they used to be).

Yet virginity is highly esteemed by God. This condition sends a message to people of every age that the satisfaction of the sexual urge doesn't contribute to the perfection of the person. That's true even though sex is not a shameful thing; it's a divine gift, ordained to life, to love, to fruitfulness.

Being a virgin — unlike, say, being black or short or gay — is a universal (not to mention invisible) human condition. Virginity refers not merely to a physiological or external fact, but more to a quality, an inner attitude. So a virgin isn't only a person (man or woman) who abstains from sexual intercourse, but one who matures to wholeness as a complete human being and is liberated — not subject to any other human being or anything else — so as to be free to serve God. Yet whereas, for some, what passes for virginity paves the way to a self-serving bachelor- or spinster-hood, for others, like Mary, true virginity gives one's all out of love and commitment, at the expense of self.

Many people discriminate against virgins. The United States is now a place where sexual modesty is actively repudiated and the woman who voluntarily abstains from sex may be regarded as repressed, socially maladjusted, or unhealthily obsessed with her father. Today men expect to be able to treat all women like prostitutes, but with barely any compensation. We have a generation of frightened, unhappy, overmedicated young women having too much sex too soon, and — worse — having it like a man: that is, having sex that is indiscriminate and loveless. The new sex-equality ethos is exacting a terrible psychic price: soaring rates of sexual harassment, date rape, and stalking.

Girls may no longer be constrained by corsets, but they are girdled nonetheless by a crippling obsession with their bodies. Although girls have always been self-conscious about their looks, the anxiety has intensified. In the early 1900's, for instance, young women rarely mentioned appearance as a source of identity, but by that century's end good bodies, rather than good characters, came to define the good self. The proliferation of mirrors and adolescent girls' dreams inspire a morbid fixation on skin and body care.

If virginity was Mary's plan, why would she become betrothed? For several reasons. There was, for one thing, the tyranny of established custom — "either marriage or the grave," said her contemporaries. In that tradition, the Jews took seriously God's first command to humankind after the creation of Adam and Eve: that they be fertile and multiply (Gn 1:28). More importantly, Mary's betrothal wasn't to just anybody, but to Joseph. He could have been of the same mind as she in reconciling the vow of virginity with marriage. Marrying, in this sense, would have been a protection to her vow.

Holy purity like Mary's is by no means a negative virtue: *don't* do this and *don't* do that. It has to do with *giving one's heart to God*. It's a *joyful affirmation*. Mary's words of surrender are beautiful, revealing the true liberated spirit: she's the maidservant of the Lord.

We who now read the story of Mary know that everything was going to turn out all right. At this point, however, Mary didn't know that. Nevertheless, we can be sure that even if she had known what she would suffer as Jesus' mother, she would have responded with the same "yes." We marvel at the incredible courage and indomitable spirit of this young woman who said "yes" to God.

That "yes" risked everything Mary had a right to hold dear: her family, her friends, her security, her respectability. But risks must be taken. People who risk nothing for God and others have nothing and are nothing. Such people may avoid suffering and sorrow, but they can't feel, grow, or love.

Theodore Roosevelt spoke well of risk and effort (*Citizenship in a Republic*, April 23, 1910): "It is not the critic who counts; not the one who points out how the strong man stumbled, or how the doer of deeds could have done them better. The credit belongs to the person who is actually in the arena; whose face is matted with dust and sweat and blood; who strives valiantly; who errs, and comes up short again and again; who knows the great enthusiasms, the great devotions, and spends himself in a worthy cause; who, if he wins, knows the triumph of high achievement; and who, if he fails, at least fails while daring greatly; so that his place shall never be with those cold and timid souls who know neither victory nor defeat."

Let's live Advent with the same spirit of service as Mary in her time of expectant waiting. May our hearts, with complete generosity, be ready to receive God's requests, His counsels, and His suggestions.

December 21

Sg 2:8-14 (or Zp 3:14-18); Lk 1:39-45

The Warmth of Giving

In this Earth's northern hemisphere, today is the shortest day and the longest night of the year. The day's cold and darkness are alleviated by the warmth and light of today's liturgy.

That warmth begins with our first reading, from the Song of Solomon (or Song of Songs or Canticle of Canticles, as it's often called). The dialogue between a woman, a man, and the Daughters of Jerusalem presents several themes common to all love literature: lovesickness, the beloved's name, obstacles to love, uniqueness. In today's portion, the main speaker is the woman. Although the literal sense of the Song is the expression of human sexual love, there's another dimension: that love isn't to be viewed apart from divine love, as the biblical symbolism of marriage indicates. The mutuality and fidelity between lovers, the goodness and sensuousness of their relationship, and their devotion to each other clearly emerge from the Song.

The woman recalls her lover paying a springtime visit. She compares the speed of her lover's approach (v. 8) to the speed of animals. The description of Spring (vv. 11-13) is the most beautiful tribute to nature in the Jewish Scriptures. There's a picturesque succession: season, blossoms, singing, figs, vines in bloom. In the end (v. 14), her lover finds her inaccessible "in the clefts of the rock" and wants to see and hear her.

The gospel shows us that Mary, too, was a lover. Having heard the voice of her divine Beloved, she immediately went to share her delight with her cousin Elizabeth; it's the nature of love to overflow, to share itself freely.

From Nazareth in Galilee, where Mary lived, to Ain Karem, about five miles west of Jerusalem, where Elizabeth lived, was about ninety miles, more than a tough four-day journey on foot. The roads and paths were full of landslides, rocks, cloudbursts, brooks without bridges, holes, snakes, scorpions, and robbers — and, of course, there were no hotels. Mary showed her unselfishness not only by quickly facing that trip with eagerness to be of help: she was also willing to stay in the background, loyal to God's wishes, obediently accepting all the uncertainties without asking why.

When these two mothers-to-be visited (v. 40), two worlds

met — not worlds of space, but of time. Elizabeth, advanced in years, symbolized the approaching end of the Age of the Mosaic Law. Her son John the Baptist would herald the new age of salvation which Israel had long awaited and which Mary now represented. In the Visitation, promise greeted fulfillment, and both Mary and Elizabeth responded to the Holy Spirit.

Though it was Elizabeth's husband Zechariah's house where they met, and Mary's dignity was the greater, it was Mary who eagerly and with youthful impetuosity greeted Elizabeth. Her greeting exuded all the warmth of a relative's affection as well as a deference to age that is so becoming for the young.

Shining out from the meeting was radiant joy. Under the special inspiration of God, the Holy Spirit spoke through Elizabeth, and she gave high praise to Mary. Her praises showed an easy familiarity with the Jewish sacred writings and echoed the praises given to Israel's heroines of old.

Elizabeth gave voice to her awareness that the infant in her womb leaped for joy (v. 44). Later, when a woman in a crowd would be so overjoyed by Jesus' words that she would cry out, "Blessed is the womb that carried you" (Lk 11:27), Jesus would reply, "Rather, blessed are those who hear the word of God and observe it" (Lk 11:28). As St. Augustine said of Mary, "It's a greater thing for her that she was Christ's disciple than that she was his mother." Mary had in her prayerful heart truly heard God's word and kept it. She was to be surprised by what God would do with her generous obedience.

Mary had beyond measure the stimulating generosity and spirit of self-giving that we commemorate at Christmastime. She put all she had at God's disposal. In an instant, all her personal plans — and undoubtedly she had some — were done with, so that she could do everything God wanted of her. Among the few gospel episodes that refer to her, two illustrate directly her attention to the wants of others. One is today's gospel, which tells us how she generously gave of herself to look after her cousin

Elizabeth until the birth of Elizabeth's son. The other was when she was generously solicitous for the well-being of the young couple at the wedding reception in Cana. Such attitudes were second nature to her.

Why shouldn't we be as generous in our response to the generosity of God? As the anonymous poet put it: "If God gave us only one day or one night, it would have been generous of Him. If God gave us only one Springtime or one Fall, one Summer or Winter, it would have been generous. If God gave us only one day of laughter, it would have been generous. If God gave us only one friend to share the journey of time, it would have been generous. If God let us laugh only once in the face of calamity, it would have been generous. If God gave us only one moment's pride in the success of those whom we love, it would have been generous. BUT He has given us life and time, joy and sorrow, sunshine and storms, laughter and tears, gifts to share and days to remember. He has given us friends, children, and parents, and Himself as well. It's God who gives us life, who tells us ever after to choose life. It's God who is our resurrection and our hope, who dwells within our hearts as the spirit of life, the vanquisher of death, and the comforter of the faithful."

In Mary we ratify the truth that generosity is a virtue of great souls who know how to find their reward in the act of giving. A generous person knows how to be loving and understanding and how to give without demanding love or understanding in return. Such persons realize that to love is in its essence to give oneself to others.

Giving enlarges the heart and makes it youthful, with an ever-greater capacity for loving. Selfishness, on the other hand, impoverishes the heart and narrows it. Selfishness is like a poison that acts slowly but with deadly effect. Each time we give ourselves exclusively to our own plans while ignoring God, we die a little more.

Generosity to God must be shown by generosity to our fellow human beings: Jesus says that as long as we did it to one of the least, we did it to him (Mt 25:40). Our Lady wasn't only generous with God in the highest degree, but also with everyone she encountered.

It's a characteristic of generosity to know how to smile and make life more agreeable for those around us; to give others the benefit of the doubt; to do the least pleasant tasks first in our work or family life; to accept people as they are without attaching too much importance to their defects; to be ready with a pat on the back for a job well done; to give a positive tone to conversations; to avoid negative criticism; to open up wider horizons, both human and supernatural. Whoever is generous out of love for Jesus isn't only enriched a hundredfold in this life, but is also destined to a reward whose munificence defies the imagination. Hard as it may sometimes seem, we can't go wrong by imitating Mary in yielding completely to God.

For those who choose the prophecy of Zephaniah as the first reading, it's good to remember that it, like the Song of Songs, announces the end of a difficult period in Israel's history. The people are asked not to fear, because God is with them; for His part, God rejoices over them, renews them in His love, and celebrates over them with loud singing. What a festival!

Although Zephaniah is generally considered a book of gloom, today's passage is a summons to rejoicing (vv. 14f.) and an edict of reassurance to Jerusalem (vv. 16f.). The summons to rejoicing has its setting in escape from defeat, as at the raising of a siege. The expression "Fear not" (v. 16) usually accompanies assurance of Yahweh's presence to save.

December 22

1 S 1:24-28; Lk 1:46-56

Two Strong Women

Our being happy may sometimes be expressed in spontaneous singing that can burst forth in seemingly incongruous times and places like the bath or while driving. Our joy is doubled if another joins us. In today's liturgy, we join Hannah the mother of Samuel, and Mary the mother of Jesus, in their songs of joy.

The baby Samuel was God's gift to a woman who had been sterile in a culture that measured a woman's worth by her ability to produce children. In return for this gift, as soon as her son was weaned Hannah gave him — this child of long desires and fervent prayer — to God's service. Hannah's song of joy and praise is the responsorial psalm in today's liturgy.

With Mary, we can well imagine the embarrassment of the increasingly obvious pregnancy of the unmarried "handmaid of the Lord." But that was the least of her worries. Would she, a mere girl, be up to the enormous responsibility of bringing into the world the "Son of the Most High" (Lk 1:32), as the angel had called him at God's invitation to her?

Every human pregnancy includes a certain anticipatory wondering and selfless hope on behalf of the child who will be taking on the journey of life. With what concern must Mary have prayed for the child growing within her!

Mary's beautiful song recorded in today's gospel, which she prayed while visiting her aged cousin Elizabeth during Elizabeth's pregnancy with John the Baptist, has come to be called her Magnificat. "Magnificat" is close to "magnify," which means to make larger. The entire poem dwells primarily on the greatness of God. Three concepts dominate: praise, thanksgiving, and joy. Many Christmas carols echo her feelings for what God does in sending Jesus.

Mary's Magnificat is modeled upon Hannah's canticle, but it also depends on the long hymnic tradition of Israel which even preexisted Hannah. Mary's words in her Magnificat show her hardly as a quiet and passive recipient of God's grace. Like a revolutionary, she proclaimed God's goodness for feeding the hungry and driving the rich away empty. Mary's song reveals her loveliness — not a soft, mushy loveliness, but a loveliness that contains revolutions.

Yes, revolutions. Not one, but several. Mary says that God has dispersed the arrogant of mind and heart (v. 51). This is the beginning of the *moral* revolution which even today is nowhere near completion. So high is the moral standard God asks of us that we need models to help us achieve it. For our moral model we can do no better than Mary. She's passionately holy and, as she shows in her Magnificat, truly humble.

The virtue of humility, so evident in Mary's life, is truth — the recognition of what we're worth in the eyes of God and of our fellow human beings. It's also an emptying of ourselves to allow God to work in us with His grace.

Humility should never be confused, however, with timidity, faint-heartedness, or mediocrity. Humility isn't opposed to the awareness of the talents we've received, nor to the full use of them with proper motivation, for humility doesn't diminish, but broadens, one's outlook. There's no possibility of sanctity without an effective struggle to acquire this virtue; without it, it's not possible even to develop an authentic human personality.

Humility gives charity consistency and makes it possible. As St. Augustine said (*On Virginity*, 51), the dwelling place of charity is humility. And St. Francis de Sales wrote (*Letters*) that these two virtues, humility and charity, are the mother virtues; the others follow as chickens do a mother hen.

Humility prevents us from letting ourselves be propelled by vanity into a mad scramble for higher and higher positions for which, perhaps, we haven't the competence, and which later on will lead to humiliation. This doesn't mean, however, that God hasn't called us to make the best use of our talents.

Mary then asserts that God has thrown down the rulers from their thrones but lifted up the lowly (v. 52). This is the beginning of a *social* revolution — again, barely begun and certainly not yet over. We hear the mouthing of politicians and others about helping the underprivileged, but not much seems to get done outside the Christmas and voting seasons — the fault of all who don't force those in power to act. Christians often forget Jesus' radical identification of himself with the lowest of the low. In this social revolution Mary, an example of concern and of putting herself out, is again a model.

Lastly, Mary says that God has filled the hungry with good things and sent the rich away empty (v. 53). This is indicative of the *economic* revolution started by Christianity — also hardly begun today. In the economic world, it's pretty much all people for themselves, getting and spending. Christians, though, should always accept their role in building a society in which, as Pope John Paul II said, "none are so poor that they have nothing to give and none are so rich that they have nothing to receive."

Unfortunately, the popular piety of Catholics has gotten away from the gospel portrait of this firebrand called Mary. Our statues and pictures portray a delicate, fair-skinned and often blue-eyed young virgin. In actuality, her skin was probably olive-colored, her hair jet black, and her eyes sparklingly dark, like most women in the Middle East today.

In today's readings both Hannah and Mary spoke and acted with exceptional strength of character and quiet composure. Hannah presented her child Samuel to the high priest Eli to minister at the sanctuary. Mary would lose her child to a servant-ministry that would lead to the cross. Yet out of each loss God created new life in unsuspecting ways. Through Samuel, God would anoint David as king and institute the royal dynasty from which Jesus would come. Through Jesus, God's kingdom would reach out to embrace the world.

Hannah and Mary help to prepare us for Christmas. As we prepare for the birth of Christ, it's a good time to reflect on the expected effects of that transition in our lives: perhaps in letting go of resentments or overcoming an unwillingness to forgive, or in helping us to affirm others rather than criticizing them or boasting about ourselves. Singing our own song of joy, thanksgiving, and praise — in the bath, on the road, or anywhere else — would be a fitting way to join Mary and Hannah in their joyous songs to God.

December 23

Ml 3:1-4, 23f.; Lk 1:57-66

Purifying Ourselves for Christmas

Which color best represents purity? Little girls receiving their first Holy Communion wear white, as do brides. Yet in the Orient white is a sign of mourning. In our Western world the color that represents purity could very well be red: the word "pure" comes from the ancient classical Greek word *pur*, meaning "fire." To purify something is to burn out its imperfections, as a refiner burns out the impurities from gold or silver.

In today's first reading, the prophet Malachi (an anonymous author whose name means "My Messenger") warns us that the Lord's coming will be painful, for he's like a refiner's fire. The situation that the prophet Malachi faced was that those who ministered to God's people were going through the outward motions of worship, but their hearts weren't in it. God wanted to purify them. Elijah, the first promised purifier, was noted for his uncompromising commitment to Yahweh and so is the ideal figure to indicate the failures of the people in their living out of their faith. His work is that of reconciliation, turning the hearts of children to their fathers and of Israel to Yahweh.

In a text put to stirring music by Handel, this third and last chapter of the prophet Malachi foretells John the Baptist's austere purifying. There's a sense of awe and majesty in the passage: the person whose coming is awaited is "a refiner and purifier" who will make his people worthy. Malachi reenacts a vision of sacrificial fire that can burn away impurities, with divine messengers and awesome people like the prophet Elijah, who long ago was taken up into heaven in a whirlwind.

For us, the joyful conclusion of that prophecy begins in earnest with today's gospel: the birth of John the Baptist. Why did Jesus need anybody to bear witness to him? Wouldn't his words and actions speak for themselves? No doubt they did, but the first step in any enterprise is always the hardest. It's very hard to go as a missionary to a strange country and try to build up a church from scratch. It's much easier to take over even a tiny church and build it up. John the Baptist gives Jesus something to build on.

The Baptist's birth is a signal that the messenger has arrived: the messenger to prepare the way of the Lord. John's birth fulfills the prophecy of Malachi that God would send Elijah the prophet before the "great and terrible day." John was a second Elijah: totally dedicated to God, and speaking words of judgment and repentance.

The last time Zechariah, the Baptist's father, had spoken, he had momentarily doubted God's promise that a child would be born to him and his wife in their old age. For his disbelief he was struck mute. Now, with his son's circumcision, his tongue was loosed and he used it to praise God.

Circumcision was very important. It may be related to human sacrifice, which was widespread in some ancient Mideast cultures (including, at some periods, the Jews) as a way of supplicating the gods. Circumcision may take the place of human sacrifice. A part of the body is substituted for the whole. Because an intimate relationship was seen between individuals and the entire community or tribe, circumcision, involving part of the male organ of procreation, proclaimed that the whole nation, the whole clan, present and future, was consecrated to the God it worshiped. It's easy to see why the descendants of Abraham came to view circumcision as a fitting and necessary expression of their covenant with the God of Israel.

The people throughout the Jewish Scriptures gave great importance to naming a child. They were mindful that the name children are given is the name by which God will call them into eternity. People at that time more generally preferred to give a son his grandfather's name, to avoid confusion. But since Zechariah was so old, any possible confusion would not be of long standing. When their neighbors and relatives expressed the expectation that the boy would be named after his father, his mother Elizabeth answered that the boy's name was to be John (v. 60); probably her husband Zechariah had made that known to her from the message of the angel (Lk 1:13).

Today, close to Christmas, we remind ourselves that the function of all we do — priests, parishioners, liturgies — is, like the function of John the Baptist, to prepare ourselves and the world for Jesus. Louis Pasteur once said, "Chance favors only the prepared mind." Of the many examples, here are a few.

One day in 1826 John Walker, a pharmacist, was mixing potassium chlorate and antimony sulfide together with a stick. The mixture stuck to the stick. When he tried to scrape the material off against the stone floor, it burst into flames. Thus did John Walker's prepared mind give birth to matches.

One day in 1839 a failed hardware salesman, Charles Goodyear at his boardinghouse in Woburn, Massachusetts, was doggedly trying to make a useful material out of a substance from

Brazil called rubber. People bought it for erasing — "rubbing" out mistakes. Because it became brittle in the cold and melted in high heat, erasing was about all it was good for. One day Goodyear blended rubber with sulfur and accidentally dropped the mixture onto a hot stove. The rubber suddenly became more solid, yet was still flexible. He had vulcanized rubber, a process that gives it useful properties, such as strength, elasticity, and stability. Today, due to the prepared Mr. Goodyear, rubber is used in everything from automobile tires to golf balls.

The switching system that led to the dial telephone was invented in 1888 by an undertaker with a problem. Almon Strowger's Kansas City funeral parlor was losing out to a competitor with an unfair advantage. The other undertaker's wife was a telephone operator. Since every phone call had to be placed by an operator in those days, she, one of the first people in town to hear about a death, would inform her husband. So Strowger, to replace human intermediaries, invented electromechanical switches to direct calls.

One day in 1928 some mold drifted through an open window in a London hospital and landed in Dr. Alexander Fleming's petri dish, where he'd placed a culture of staphylococcus bacteria. When he looked through the microscope, he saw the mold efficiently destroying the germs. Fleming received a Nobel Prize in 1945 for inventing penicillin.

One day shortly after World War II, Percy Lebaron Spencer was walking through his lab at the Raytheon Company in Cambridge, Massachusetts, when he stopped briefly by a magnetron — the tube that produces the high-frequency microwaves that power radar. He realized that a candy bar in his jacket pocket had just melted. Thus the prepared Dr. Spencer gave birth to the microwave oven.

All these people were prepared for what happened. As preparation for Jesus' coming, and in the spirit of John the Baptist let's prepare ourselves to bring home more profoundly to ourselves the love and depth of God's new relationship with humanity that began on the first Christmas.

December 24

2 S 7:1-5, 8-12, 16; Lk 1:67-79

He's Almost Here!

This day before Christmas, we celebrate the fact that God is about to break into our lives with overwhelming goodness. We feel almost giddy with joy. The greatest of thinkers, from Aristotle on, have tackled the problem of what's funny, which has a knack of baffling every effort. Unfortunately, Aristotle's treatise on laughter was lost in history. And humor is very hard to explain.

How the body laughs is well understood. Amusement initiates the coordinated action of fifteen facial muscles, beginning with a lift of the eyebrows and a series of eye- and cheek-muscle contractions. What follows are spasmodic skeletal muscle contractions, a quickened heartbeat, and rapid breathing. The diaphragm contracts in clonic movements that crescendo and diminish. However, how the brain processes humor remains a mystery. It's easy to make someone smile or cry by electronically stimulating a single region of the brain, but it's astonishingly difficult to make someone laugh.

As David in our first reading came to realize, we know that God needs none of our actions. Ever since God brought the Israelites out of Egypt, He had dwelt in a tent. Though David was totally in need of the Lord, God had no need of a proper dwelling place as conceived by David. Instead of a glorious building, God promised to dwell with David and his dynasty forever.

God's plan, communicated by Nathan, endorsed all the

blessings given by God to David, but denied him the privilege of building a Temple. The royal dynasty was unconditionally blessed by God, from which blessing came the messianic hope of Israel and the Savior Jesus, Son of David.

Many forces were at work in God's rejecting David's request to build a Temple. One was the fact that for two or three hundred years, Mosaic religion centered in the ark of the covenant, enshrined within a nomad's tent. This tent could easily be collapsed and carried by the people in their wanderings. At the people's supreme moment of prayer, God wasn't to be dependent upon human wealth, status, or rank; a Temple with mighty walls and glistening splendor might destroy the sense of faith.

When the angel Gabriel had come from God to Zechariah with the news of Elizabeth's impending pregnancy, it was, nevertheless, to a Temple that had been built by David's son Solomon, where Zechariah was serving as a priest. Zechariah found it hard to believe that two old people like himself and his wife Elizabeth would have a child as promised by the angel.

As a result of Zechariah's disbelief, the angel had given Zechariah a sign: he wouldn't be able to speak until the birth of his son. Today's gospel contains his song of praise when Elizabeth gave birth to a son, and Zechariah's speech returned. His song of praise — the *Benedictus*, it's called from its first word in Latin — is full of allusions to the promises of the Jewish Scriptures now being fulfilled in his son John.

The *Benedictus*, the great prophetic song of the New Testament, begins by Zechariah blessing God. Then he plumbs the depths of Old Testament prophecy, bringing up promise after promise which God has now fulfilled by His great act of deliverance: God has now visited His people, He has come to their rescue, He has raised up a power for salvation. It's fitting that the Church has appointed this great song to be proclaimed every morning in the Divine Office, so that we can be daily reminded that Jesus has visited us, giving light to those who live in darkness and the shadow of death, guiding our feet into the way of peace.

Whereas the royal House of David lasted for many hundreds of years, one of the most successful of all earthly dynasties, it had come to an end when Judah was taken into exile by the King of Babylon. In Jesus, born into the House of David, a kingdom of this world becomes the Kingdom of God.

It's often said that our celebration of Jesus' birth, Christmas, is for children. Children do give Christmas a special spice — but what do they know? A Sunday school class of first-graders was asked by their teacher to put on a play about their own version of the Nativity. They had the familiar cast: Joseph, the Three Wise Men, the star, and an angel in the background. Everything else was modernized. There were some bales of straw, behind which Mary was apparently in labor. Suddenly the "doctor" emerged from the "delivery room" with a big smile and the surprise announcement: "Congratulations, Joseph, it's a God!"

We're impressed by divine surprises. Surprises happen in our lives every day. Just as no sunrise is ever exactly the same as the day before, God never comes the same way into our lives. There's a ceaseless variation of details: people come and go, physical activities are in flux, and mental peace has its ebb and flow. In this ever-changing canvas of our lives, where the ink always flows into new colors and directions, God comes. Over and over again He's born, as our lives take a fresh start.

In truth, there's no end to the age when we can enjoy Christmas. Minimally, a proper celebration of it would renew our conviction that the reason for all the excitement and joy is that the Light of the World and the Prince of Peace comes to everybody — young, old, and in between. So to everyone, of all ages, a Merry Christmas!

CHRISTMAS SEASON

Jesus and Santa Claus

According to the Church, the most famous people we commemorate in the Advent season are the prophet Isaiah, the Virgin Mary, St. Joseph, and St. John the Baptist, as well as the coming baby Jesus. In today's world, however, the most famous people of Advent and Christmas are Santa Claus and — sometimes — Jesus.

In the Christian tradition Santa Claus's name is really Saint Nicholas. "Santa Claus" is after the Dutch "Sinter Claes." He was probably the Bishop of Myra in Asia Minor, now Turkey, in the early fourth century. (According to Acts 21:1, St. Paul visited Patara, and some texts add "and Myra.") He's become the patron saint of children, of sailors (whom he reportedly saved off the coast of Lycia), of charitable fraternities and guilds, of cities such as Fribourg (in Switzerland) and Moscow, as well as such countries as Russia and Greece. Numerous surnames of people are derived from Nicholas (for example, Nichols, Nicholson, Colson, Collins). Thousands of churches are dedicated to him.

An early story links Nicholas to the tradition of gift-giving. It's said that in Myra lived a family with three daughters so poor they didn't have enough money for even one dowry, so none of them could marry. The eldest volunteered to sell herself into slavery and prostitution to earn a dowry for the other two. Nicholas heard of this and anonymously sent three gifts of money to the family over three years, allowing the three daughters to marry, one after another.

The first time he did it, the money was said to have been thrown over a garden wall in a purse that landed down the daughters' chimney — creating the popular myth about Santa Claus and chimneys. Another time the purse, after being thrown over the wall, became tangled with clothes on a wash line; hence the connection with Christmas stockings.

Santa Claus is a symbol that grew in New York City. Two men were especially responsible. Clement Clarke Moore, a prominent Protestant theologian, became famous for a little poem which he (or, as some say, Henry Livingston, Jr.) wrote for his six children. That poem, "A Visit from St. Nicholas," written in 1822, began "'Twas the night before Christmas." In it, Moore helped create Santa as "a right jolly old elf" who arrives with a clatter in a sleigh pulled by eight flying reindeer.

The second man responsible for the transformation of Santa Claus was Thomas Nast, the cartoonist. He illustrated Moore's poem in 1860 for *Harper's Weekly*. He furthered the imaginative overhaul of the saint from the gaunt, grave judge of good and bad behavior of the Dutch tradition to the huggable: cheeks round, ruddy, and dimpled; white-haired; bearded; wearing a bright red suit trimmed in white fur; and with a big, booming laugh. In one hand he held a long-stem pipe.

Nast drew Santa at work in an ice palace and later specifically identified it as the North Pole — his one totally original touch in Santa's evolution. Once the sleigh was established as his mode of transport, the snowy north as his home was inevitable. The North Pole made another kind of sense: No country could claim Santa as its own. Two other familiar touches in the Santa story — the workshop and the ledger to record good and bad behavior — also came from Nast.

By the 1870's, parents and children were writing Santa and he was writing back. One letter received a famous reply. In the Summer of 1897 eight-year-old Virginia O'Hanlon, with the encouragement of her parents, childishly scrawled a letter to the *New York Sun*, saying: "Some of my friends say there is no Santa Claus. Please tell me the truth, is there a Santa Claus?"

In Francis P. Church's editorial of September 21,1897, belief in Santa personified belief in all the intangible good things about people that really did exist but couldn't be seen. His clever editorial also typified the best of Christianity.

His answer said, in part: "Yes, Virginia, there is a Santa Claus. He exists as certainly as love and generosity and devotion exist, and you know that they abound and give to your life its highest beauty and joy.... If there were no Santa Claus... there would be no... poetry, no romance to make tolerable this existence. We should have no enjoyment, except in sense and sight.... The most real things in the world are those that neither children nor men can see.... Only faith, poetry, love, romance, can... view and picture the supernal beauty and glory beyond.... Ah, Virginia, in all this world there is nothing else real and abiding." That editorial was an immediate sensation, and remains one of the most famous editorials ever written.

However, the legends about the original St. Nicholas were downgraded in 1969, when the Vatican removed him from its universal calendar of saints on the grounds it didn't have enough evidence to prove he existed.

Yet the true symbol of Christmas isn't Santa Claus, but the stable-crib. And Jesus is even better than Santa Claus. As one anonymous wise man wrote:

SANTA is about legend...
JESUS is about truth.
SANTA lives at the North Pole...
JESUS is everywhere.
SANTA rides in a sleigh...
JESUS rides on the wind and walks on the water.
SANTA comes but once a year...
JESUS is an ever-present help.
SANTA fills your stockings with goodies...
JESUS supplies all your needs.
SANTA comes down your chimney uninvited...
JESUS stands at your door and knocks, and then enters your heart when invited.
You have to wait in line to see SANTA...
JESUS is as close as the mention of his name.

SANTA lets you sit on his lap…
JESUS lets you rest in his arms.
SANTA doesn't know your name; all he can say is, "Hi little boy or girl, what's your name?"…
JESUS knew our name before we did.
SANTA has a belly like a bowl full of jelly…
JESUS has a heart full of love.
All SANTA can offer is HO HO HO…
JESUS offers health, hope, and love.
SANTA says, "You better not cry"…
JESUS says, "Cast all your cares on Me for I care for you."
SANTA'S little helpers make toys…
JESUS makes new life, mends wounded hearts, repairs broken homes, and builds mansions.
SANTA may make you chuckle, but…
JESUS gives you joy that is your strength.
While SANTA puts gifts under your tree…
JESUS became our gift and died on a tree.
It's obvious there is really no comparison:
JESUS is still the reason for the season. Yes,
JESUS is better. He is even better than Santa Claus.

That comparison between Santa and Jesus makes it obvious that we need to put Christ back in CHRISTmas. The two holidays that celebrate the divinity of Christ are Easter and Christmas. Two popular songs have taken Christ out of them both: "Easter Parade" and "I'm Dreaming of a White Christmas." One turns Easter into a fashion show and the other turns Christmas into a holiday about snow.

The secularization of Christmas continues in the United States, and can be expected to accelerate as millions of non-Western, non-Christian people pour into this country. Department store employees are instructed not to say "Merry Christmas"; "Happy Holidays" becomes the proverbial greeting. School calendars dub Christmas vacation the "Winter Holiday"; in school children sing songs about reindeer; the Christmas tree becomes an artificial religious symbol; instead of designating the centuries by B.C. and A.D., we're urged to use C.E. (Common Era) and B.C.E. (Before the Common Era).

In protest against the commercialization of Christmas, a group in Innsbruck in Austria asked stores to replace window displays of Santa and his reindeer with images of the Christ Child and angels. In the United States, a professor argues that the secular side of Christmas has become a sort of religion in itself: Santa, and not Jesus, is the savior.

Some of our fellow citizens may persist in ousting God from our culture to the extent that we won't even be able to say "God bless you" when someone sneezes. And at Christmas we'll be able to wish each other only a "Merry Mishmash."

But Christians will never forget that Christmas is the story of Christ's birth. Christmas is, for one thing, an event of light. For sinners, it dissipates the clouds of sin. For the oppressed, the suffering, and those who walk in darkness, this is the light of the new creation which radiates from the humility of the crib.

The manger is the cradle of immortal life. This is the kind of life which has totally changed history. Since Bethlehem, all humankind knows that God became human, and did so in order to give human beings a share in His divine life. So all creation is invited to rejoice with all the nations of the earth.

There's a story that illustrates the true nature of Christmas. In a public school's kindergartners' pageant, each little group, one by one, rose to do their thing. Because the public school had long stopped referring to the holiday as "Christmas," nothing was expected but songs of reindeer, Santa Claus, snowflakes, and good cheer. But this little group rose to sing, "Christmas Love."

The children were aglow, adorned in fuzzy mittens, red sweaters, and bright snowcaps. Those in the front row center of the stage held up large letters, one by one, to spell out the title of their song. As the class would sing "C is for Christmas," a child would hold up the letter C. Then "H is for Happy," and so on, until each child holding up his portion had presented the complete message, "Christmas Love."

The performance was going smoothly, until the little girl in the front row holding the letter "M" was holding it upside down, totally unaware that her letter "M" had appeared as a "W." The audience snickered at the little girl's mistake. The laughter continued, until the last letter was raised, and the audience saw it all together. A hush came over the audience and eyes began to widen. When the last letter was held high, the message read loud and clear: "CHRISTWAS LOVE." Everybody understood why they were celebrating the holiday.

Have a merry Christmas!

December 26 — St. Stephen

Ac 6:8-10; 7:54-59; Mt 10:17-22

Witness and the Gift of Forgiveness

On our own, we would never have thought to celebrate on the day after Christmas a man who was stoned to death for his belief in Christ. But celebrating St. Stephen today in the midst of all our good fellowship, fun, and family reunions reminds us that even in the Christmas celebration there can be pain. St. Fulgentius said (*Sermon* 3): "Yesterday, we wrapped Christ in swaddling clothes; today, he clothes Stephen with the garment of immortality. Yesterday, a narrow manger cradled the baby Jesus; today, the infinite heaven has received Stephen in triumph."

One reason why Stephen's feast occurs today is memorable:

St. Stephen's day is linked with the two feast days that follow it, first that of St. John the Evangelist and then that of the Holy Innocents slain by King Herod. By grouping these three feasts together and associating them with Christ's birth, the Church is marking three kinds of martyrdom, or witness: those like Stephen who choose to die for the cause, those like John who are willing to die for the cause but never actually do, and those like the Holy Innocents who die for the cause without a choice.

In today's gospel Jesus predicts that because of belief in him there would be flogging in the synagogues, and parents and their children would be going against each other. Jesus had predicted how his followers would be plotted against, hated, and persecuted unto death for his sake.

Stephen was a man of grace and strength (Ac 6:8), of sufficient inner freedom to step out from behind the security of the letter of the Mosaic Law and proclaim his vision of what the coming of the Messiah means for his people. He was one of the first seven men chosen to be deacons.

The creation of deacons came about in this way. No sooner had the number of Christians begun to grow than the Hellenist Christians complained against the Hebrew Christians. Both groups were composed of Jews — this was before non-Jews began to enter the Church. The Hellenist Christians spoke Greek, the common language of the eastern Roman Empire, and were more exposed to the wider non-Jewish culture. The Hebrew Christians spoke Aramaic and were the majority in the Church at the time.

The division was theological, cultural, and practical. The Hebrew Christians were insisting on the Temple as the sole place of Jewish sacrifice; the others were challenging the Temple's centrality. In practice, the division brought about financial results: the Hellenist Christians were of the opinion that their needy weren't getting a fair share of the community's common goods.

The leaders devised the creative solution of choosing seven

men, Stephen among them, to assure that the needs of the Hellenist Christians were met. These were the first deacons. According to the Acts of the Apostles in a few verses before today's reading, deacons were to be men of good reputation, full of the Spirit and of wisdom. As centuries passed, the function and meaning of the permanent diaconate (as contrasted with the transitional diaconate on the way to the priesthood) took various forms. It is, however, always linked to service.

Deacons are ordained ministers whose primary ministry continues to involve works of charity and social justice. They're ordained to bring the needs of the poor, the socially marginalized, and the powerless to the Church ("the assembly") and in return bring the resources of the Church to the aid of these people. Their primary involvement continues to be to such areas as (but not limited to) jails, soup kitchens, homeless and battered-person shelters, AIDS patients, and victims of racial, economic, and social oppression. Deacons and their ministry are sacramental signs of the Church's option for the poor.

The diaconate is the one ordained ministry in the Church that does not *primarily* occupy itself with liturgy or with governance, the ministries we usually associate with priests or bishops. But deacons can preach when authorized, and preside at baptisms, marriages, and burials where needed.

Deacons can have a meaningful appeal, in that most of them are married, have or had active careers in other areas of work, and have no reason to give service to the Church other than their faith commitment. The ritual prayer that commissions deacons is significant: "Receive the gospel of Christ whose herald you are; believe what you read, preach what you believe, put into practice what you preach."

Stephen's preaching inflamed Jewish ire. He continually argued, publicly and privately, that all the Hebrew Scriptures led to Jesus. His language at times was fierce, hardly adapted to calm and reasonable dialogue. For instance, he called the Sanhedrin, the highest Jewish governing body, "a stiff-necked people, uncircumcised in heart and ears."

Stephen is celebrated as the Church's first martyr. The word "martyr" means literally "witness"; and Stephen is a lesson to all of us to stand up for what's right and true — though our bearing witness is unlikely to be as hazardous as it was for him.

Stephen's audience was no more pleased at hearing his mentioning the significant term "Son of Man" — knowing its implication of the divine — than those who had heard Jesus use it. Considering it blasphemy, they shouted in fury, covered their ears to hear no more, rushed him, dragged him out of the city, and stoned him to death (Ac 7:57f.). None of this was an official act of Judaism, since in Roman times the Sanhedrin didn't have the power to put anyone to death. It was in our terms a lynching. The custom for such a lynch mob at that time and place was to lead the condemned to a height and throw him off. If that didn't kill him, they threw rocks on him until he died. In Stephen's case, the participants in this ugly activity laid down their cloaks at the feet of a young man named Saul (v. 58), the future St. Paul.

Implicitly, Stephen's prayer for the forgiveness of his infuriated audience attempted to overcome the disunity between him and them as well as between them and God. Stephen saw beyond the faces of his audience that were distorted with rage; he saw even beyond time, to the Son of Man standing at God's right hand (vv. 55f.) — a position of power and authority.

Stephen died very much as Jesus had. Both Jesus and Stephen were accused of blasphemy. Both were tried by a mob and — again in our terms — a kangaroo court. Both were taken outside the Holy City to be killed. Both died violent deaths. Both prayed to the heavenly Father to forgive their murderers. And both at the last commended their spirits to God.

Persecution still goes on. It takes many forms. Already in his time, St. Augustine wrote (*Commentary on the Psalms*, 39:1): "In former times, Christians were incited to renounce Christ; now they are taught to deny Christ. Then they were forced, now they are taught; then violence was used, now it is deception; then one heard the shouts of the enemy; now, when he prowls around, gentle and insinuating, it is difficult to recognize him."

We celebrate God's enduring love, as in the birth of Jesus at Christmas, but we also share in the sufferings of Jesus, as with the death of Stephen. In our day, disciples continue to give their lives as Stephen did. For most of us, though, that means in smaller ways, like dying to self-centeredness.

We pray that in the unjust ridicule we receive for advocating what is true and right and just — as, for example, condemning abortion and euthanasia — we shall stand as tall as Stephen. We pray for help to love our enemies, as did Stephen. We pray that in witnessing to truth we're not passive, lethargic, and indifferent, but form ourselves into a zealous people like Stephen, eager to proclaim justice. We pray that we may have courage like Stephen's to be God's witnesses. And we pray to receive Stephen's gift of being able to forgive.

December 27 — St. John the Evangelist

1 Jn 1:1-4; Jn 20:2-8

Eagerness to Find the Whole Jesus

The Church groups three feasts together after Christmas and associates them with Christ's birth: yesterday's celebration of St. Stephen, today's feast of St. John the Evangelist, and tomorrow's commemoration of the Holy Innocents. The Church is thus marking three kinds of witness, or martyrdom: those like Stephen who choose to die for a cause and so meet their death, those like John who choose to die for a cause but never actually do so, and those like the Holy Innocents who die for a cause without a choice.

St. John the Evangelist was a native of Bethsaida, a Galilean town on the northern shore of the Lake of Galilee. His parents were Zebedee and Salome and his brother was St. James the Greater — a well-to-do family of fisherfolk. James and John, when they met Our Lord, left their father Zebedee in the boat with the hired servants and followed Jesus (Mk 1:20). Salome, their mother, also followed Jesus, helping him in Galilee and Jerusalem, and accompanying him to Calvary (Mk 15:40f.).

For John (as for everyone) his new vocation gave a new meaning even to the most ordinary things of his life. The discovery of one's personal vocation changes everything without changing anything — just as a landscape, without changing, is different before the sun goes down, beneath the light of the moon, or wrapped in the darkness of night. Today, on his feast, we look at "the disciple whom Jesus loved" with a holy envy for the immense gift which the Lord bestowed upon him.

Unexpectedly in this Christmas season, today's gospel draws our attention to an important aspect of Jesus: his Resurrection. Jesus' friends couldn't visit his tomb on the Sabbath, because that would be breaking the Law of Moses, so by early Sunday morning Mary Magdalene's overpowering love for Jesus could wait no longer: when it was still dark, she went to the tomb. Finding it empty, she excitedly ran back to the city to get support and help from Peter, the leader of the Apostles, and John (v. 2).

Why Peter? By now everyone surely knew of his denial of Jesus, which had shown his weak and cowardly side. But there was another side to Peter: a quality of charismatic leadership. After his Resurrection, we now know, Jesus would place further confidence in him by telling him to feed his flock.

And why John? He was the "Beloved Disciple": he had been present at Jesus' Transfiguration; he had helped Peter prepare for Jesus' last Passover meal; he had had a place of great honor at the Last Supper; during Jesus' trial, he had helped get Peter entry to the court of the High Priest; and at the foot of the cross, Jesus had entrusted the care of his mother to him.

Inasmuch as the gospel shows the young fleet-of-foot John beating the older Peter in the excited race to Jesus' grave, perhaps the Church exercised a sense of humor in choosing this passage for today's celebration. The Beloved Disciple had learned the good news from the practical women. On arrival, the dignity of Peter had to be respected, and John stepped aside to allow Peter to enter the tomb first. Different people have different roles in discovering and proclaiming the Resurrection. Each of us has a talent for making known Jesus' message.

Perhaps the Church also wants to remind us in this season that the one whose birthday we've been celebrating is none other than the Son of God. When Peter and John arrived at the tomb, the intact burial cloths appeared to them almost as though the body had evaporated out of them. Putting everything together, the amazing truth seemed to be that Jesus had risen!

Both Peter and John saw, but John saw and believed (v. 8). Seeing isn't necessarily believing. Seeing, plus a lot of loving — these are what it takes to enable us to understand what otherwise we cannot. To know other people in their uniqueness as other persons and not merely as objects, love — not only intellection — is necessary. The Beloved Disciple illustrated Jesus' comment that it's those who have not seen and have believed who are blessed (Jn 20:29).

Today's first reading from the opening words of the First Letter of John — who may or may not be the same as the author of the gospel — seems breathlessly excited by what he's telling us. When the author of this letter proclaims "what was from the beginning," he was thinking, as did the opening lines of the gospel of John the Evangelist, of the first moments of creation. He's bearing witness to what has existed from all eternity.

Why did John begin this letter by stating that he has seen,

touched, and heard the word of life that was from the beginning? The Apostles emphasized Jesus' Resurrection and his sending his Spirit into the Church. The Holy Spirit would *enliven* people with the attitudes of Jesus, so that others could see, in the members of the Church, Christ's body, a continuation of the marvelous Christmas revelation of the word of life.

The life of each member of Christ's mystical body, then and now, was to become another revelation of Jesus. Each new grace in everyone can be compared to a new birth of Jesus. As Jesus is born anew in us, we can tenderly touch, see, and hear the word of life. We must listen carefully, for that word sometimes whispers. We must look intently, for there's an ever new revelation of life and growth. Here in the midst of the Church, the assembly of God, we possess what couldn't be contained in a manger — or within a tomb.

December 28 — Holy Innocents

1 Jn 1:5-2:2; Mt 2:13-18

Darkness Against the Light

The early morning sun shone brightly in the cemetery on the tiny wooden coffin coated in white velvet. It sat next to a heap of earth, ready for burial, among the brass plaques marking graves adorned with little rubber ducks, pacifiers, and toy Santas.

The newborn girl, Angelica, had been found dead in a bag by workers sorting through trash being trucked to a sanitation plant. So for the twelfth time in a year, Jim Jackson, a paramedic, stood graveside with a clutch of fellow paramedics, police officers, and strangers, searching for the right thing to say about a baby found in the garbage.

"She will rest in peace with the others," Jim said, his voice catching. The "others" had been tossed away, too — hurled in the trash, or suffocated in bags, or smothered in shallow graves. A motorcade had escorted the hearse from the church to the cemetery. Bagpipes cried "Amazing Grace." Crisp salutes abounded as two pallbearers, chosen at random from paramedics and their friends, carried the tiny body. As the church bells tolled, people found it a heartbreaking experience.

These babies are the modern equivalent of the innocents in Herod's time — with some differences. The babies of Herod's time had been lovingly cared for by their parents; today's babies were abandoned — abandoned by their misguided parents or because of the hardness of society. The innocents in Herod's time were murdered because a deluded ruler saw a threat in Jesus; today's innocents are abandoned because of a youth culture's bewilderment.

Further, reliable estimates say that at least 1.2 million children are trafficked worldwide each year into exploitative work. They're placed in domestic work, unregulated industrial labor, construction sites, service-sector locales such as laundries and restaurants, farming, or street activities such as hawking or begging. Many children who are trafficked for labor exploitation end up in the commercial sex trade. Children are simply easier to abuse and less able to stand up for their rights than adults. Consequently, they can be made to work longer hours with less food, poor accommodation, and no benefits.

Today's gospel shows that not even the Holy Family was spared trials and sufferings. The baby Jesus' life was threatened and the Holy Family became displaced persons in a foreign country. No matter how many or how few of St. Matthew's details are factual, he wants to show the important phenomenon of a family open to God yet vulnerable to the tide of fortune.

Through it all, St. Joseph obeyed God's revelation. He was a courageous man of honor who wanted to protect Mary's reputation, because God wanted him to; a man who married Mary even though the child with whom she was pregnant wasn't his, because God told him to; a man who, to protect his family, led them into exile, because God instructed him to.

Because Egypt bordered on the Holy Land, many Jews were finding refuge there beyond the jurisdiction of Herod. Four to five days' walking would bring them to Rhinocolura, on the Egyptian frontier. There they would meet fellow refugees. Alexandria was long a place of culture because — in part, at least — of the presence of over a million Jews. Joseph would be welcomed, and he would be able to find a livelihood in his trade of carpentry.

But the trip would be a nightmare. In Gaza, they would pick up the route of the coastal plain. Before them were the rigors of the long trek across the desert, exposed to cold nights and scorching daylight sand. Traveling by night and hiding by day, they would be able to reach the border in three or four days, and then could rest a little easier.

Meanwhile, back home things weren't going well, as the message to Joseph had foretold. Bethlehem and its outlying farms probably had about 2,000 inhabitants, so the number of boys slain by Herod "the Great" would have been between twenty and thirty. The Holy Innocents suffered quickly; it was their loving and bewildered parents who felt the most intense pain from the swords that struck their babies.

In the Greek language which he knew well, Caesar Augustus said that he would rather be Herod's pig (*hus*) than his son (*huios*), because Herod refused to eat pork while he slew his own offspring. He had inserted a barbarous provision in his will to ensure that some tears would be shed when he died: that at his death all the nobles of the kingdom be gathered into a stadium at Jericho and butchered.

The Holy Family stayed in Egypt until the death of Herod (v. 15): perhaps as long as three years. A modern medical researcher found a description of Herod's ailments in the writings of the first century historian Flavius Josephus. The researcher opined that what is now called Fournier's gangrene, rare today, probably killed Herod. He opined that Herod suffered also from kidney disease. Itching from that would have caused Herod to scratch his skin and open it to infectious bacteria, leading to gangrene. Kidney disease may also have resulted in the untreated accumulation of bodily wastes, which can result in mental illness. That in turn may explain some of Herod's brutal acts, including the executions of several family members.

When God told Joseph to go back to his own country, again he obeyed. A provision of Herod's will had divided his kingdom into three parts, one for each of his three sons Archelaus, Antipas, and Philip. Archelaus was given Judea and Samaria; he was so cruel that, to quell a civil war, he opened his rule with the deliberate slaughter of 3,000 of the most influential people in his area. In ten years the Roman emperor Augustus would have to remove him from power.

At the time of today's gospel Archelaus still ruled Judea and Samaria, which contained Bethlehem and Jerusalem. Clearly, it was unsafe for the Holy Family to settle there. Joseph therefore guided Mary and Jesus to Galilee (v. 22), where Antipas reigned. Though Antipas was the one who would execute John the Baptist and before whom Jesus would be arraigned, it was safe, at least for now, to settle in Nazareth (v. 23).

The gospel's allusion to Rachel refers (Jr 31:15) to this favorite wife of the patriarch Jacob, who longed for a child. Only after many years did she conceive, but then she died in giving birth. With her last breath she called her son Ben-oni ("son of my affliction"), but his father named him Benjamin ("son of my right hand" — Gn 35:18). Matthew poetically represents Rachel as mourning for her descendants, who would be taken away into exile.

Suffering is a reality in life. There's no easy explanation for it, least of all for the suffering of the innocent. Though suffering is a mystery, faith can help us discover in the darkness of our own or other people's suffering the loving and provident hand of our Father God who knows so much more and sees so much farther than we can.

For the Holy Innocents, the agony was soon over; in the next world they would come to know for all eternity the one whom they had died to save. For their parents, the pain lasted longer; but at death they found that there was a special sense in which God was in their debt.

Today's excerpt from St. John's First Letter challenges us to live in the light. That means living in a truthful relationship with God, with others, and especially with ourselves. As we shape our lives, so we shape our world. Let's pray that children come to appreciate the sacrifices their parents make for them and overcome the temptations which might lead them from the path of virtue. Most of all, let's remember the example of the Holy Family.

December 29 — Fifth Day in the Octave of Christmas

1 Jn 2:3-11; Lk 2:22-35

More Early Witnesses to the Baby in the Crèche

We have the ability today to make our homes the best they've ever been. The attributes of home "comfort" — privacy, intimacy, domesticity, ease, leisure, pleasure, convenience — only gradually combined over about the last 200 years to create a sense of "home" that we take for granted. If our families aren't what they should be, it's one of the greatest tragedies of the Western world — ever!

The ancient Jews knew instinctively that a good family life must be centered not in comfort, but in a deep reverence for God. Today's section of St. Luke's gospel tells of typical ceremonies in the life of a Jewish family. One of the ceremonies took place at the presentation of a baby in the Temple — the ritual whereby parents dedicated their newborn to God. Christians have made the presentation of the baby Jesus a joyful mystery of the rosary, because it gave Mary and Joseph joy to present their child to God.

Another Jewish ceremony was purification after childbirth. After giving birth, a mother was held to be ritually unclean. She was to offer two gifts to God in the Temple. One was a lamb in thanksgiving for the birth of her child, the other a young pigeon to remove her ritual uncleanness. If a family couldn't afford the lamb, they were permitted to offer another pigeon instead (Lv 12:8). This offering of two pigeons came to be called the Offering of the Poor. Luke's "Gospel of the Poor" mentions (v. 24) that this was the offering of Mary and Joseph. It showed that they were lower middle class at best, having no luxuries, sacrificing to make ends meet, accounting for every penny spent, and knowing the insecurity of life.

Though these ceremonies may seem strange to us, behind them lies a recognition of what many have lost sight of: that a child is a gift of God and that, of all God's gifts, there is none for which people shall be held more accountable.

In the Temple, the Holy Family met a man who was among the few who didn't go along with Jewish dreams of armies or power, believing instead in a life of prayer to discern God revealing His plans. He was the devout Simeon: the quiet man, the man who listens. As a result of listening to the Holy Spirit, he came into the Temple (v. 27).

He held the baby, whom through prayer he recognized as

the salvation of God, in his arms; then he told God that he was ready to depart this life in peace, his words echoing the prophecies found in Isaiah's "Book of Consolation." How heroic is Simeon's desire! Most people are afraid to die. Yet in Simeon's view lies all hope for life and goodness.

At Jesus' birth, Mary and Joseph in their loneliness had been astonished that the shepherds and the Magi should come; now they gasped to think that this stranger not only knew their child, but knew something of his future (v. 33). In fact, Simeon proceeded to give his mother a summary of Jesus' fate (vv. 34f.). That Jesus would be for the rise of many, Mary found easy to accept. It was, however, hard for her to believe that her baby would be the downfall of anyone. We, too, would wonder how that could be. There are some, however, who would reject this child, the Redeemer of the world. By one's stand toward Jesus one lays bare one's heart (v. 35).

Capping Simeon's words was his prophecy that Mary would be pierced with a sword. To her, God was a loving Father who permits us to be tested to show who we are. Her willingness to accept whatever came — including, if that be God's will, a sword — gave an inkling of who she is.

Today's selection from the First Letter of St. John tells us that the Son of God took on human flesh in order to fill us with divine life. John emphasizes our seeing this divine life in our fellow human beings. Without love for our brothers and sisters, says John, our claim to the dignity of divine life is a lie; to claim to be in the light while hating others means we're still in darkness. The test is how we treat others. No true Christian can dismiss another human being as of no worth.

The "new" quality, added by John to the "old" commandment, comes from the presence of Jesus. No true follower of Jesus can bypass the extraordinary way by which Jesus has extended our primary human obligation of charity, forgiveness, and patience. Jesus presents these norms not as a nice ideal, nor as a yardstick for correct etiquette, but as a command for every one of his followers.

To fulfill our calling may be difficult but, as a wise man (Robert Louis Stevenson) said, "Don't judge each day by the harvest you reap but by the seeds you plant." A good example of that is Thomas Becket. He was born in London in 1118. A cleric of the diocese of Canterbury, he first became chancellor to the king and then in 1162 was chosen bishop. His tireless defense of the rights of the Church against King Henry II prompted the king to exile him to France for six years. After returning to his homeland, he endured many trials and in 1170 was murdered by agents of the king.

In a letter, Thomas Becket as bishop wrote (as in the *Divine Office* for this day): "[N]o matter who plants or waters, God gives no harvest unless what he plants is the faith of Peter, and unless he himself assents to Peter's teaching. All important questions that arise among God's people are referred to the judgment of Peter in the person of the Roman Pontiff.... Remember... the sufferings through which the Church has grown, and the storms the ship of Peter has weathered because it has Christ on board. Remember how the crown was attained by those whose sufferings gave new radiance to their faith. The whole company of saints bears witness to the unfailing truth that without real effort no one wins the crown."

December 30 —
Sixth Day in the Octave of Christmas

1 Jn 2:12-17; Lk 2:36-40

Lessons from Jerusalem and Nazareth

Yesterday's gospel introduced us to Mary and Joseph abiding by typical ceremonies in the life of a Jewish family of that time: the presentation of a newborn child in the Temple and offering him to God. That gospel spoke of their meeting Simeon there. Today, St. Luke's gospel introduces us to another person whom the Holy Family met there: the prophetess Anna.

The devout Anna was similar to the many women who often form the core of the faithful at daily worship in our churches today. Luke knows her name, her father's name, her tribe, her age, her marital status, her life story, and her present way of life.

After only seven years of marriage, she became a widow (v. 37). Modern widows have commented that typical of early widowhood is loss of self-esteem, nonacceptance by married friends who feel uncomfortable socializing with a single widow, and worries about finances. Some widows say that initially they're so exhausted by grief that they can hardly get out of bed in the morning.

Anna's being a widow meant that, at least because of the death of her husband, she had known sorrow. Sorrow can make us hard, bitter, and resentful, or more understanding, kinder, and more sympathetic. It can take away our faith or make our faith more solid. Which of these alternatives happens will depend on what we think about God — whether He's a tyrant who sends sorrows with no apparent reason other than His own pleasure, or a loving Father who permits us to be tested to show who we are. To Anna, God was a loving Father.

She was eighty-four years old (v. 37). Age can do worse than sap one's bodily strength: it can take away our heart, so that we become grimly resigned to the way things are. On the other hand, it can also give us wisdom and humor and other virtues. With regard to humor as being essential to a family, in a cartoon a wife turns to her husband whose face is buried in the newspaper and says: "The marriage counselor told me to complement you more often.... Hey, nice elbows!"

Here again, how we develop will depend on what we think of God. If we conceive Him to be distant and remote, we despair. If He's intimately connected with our life, we have hope. Anna, despite her age, hadn't stopped hoping. Luke tells us how she managed to stay like that: she was in constant contact with the Source of all strength through prayer. That's as good a prescription for a "fountain of youth" as all the exercise programs and diet manuals on the market.

Her values were different from those of the "world," of which today's reading from the First Letter of St. John speaks. The "world" is a word that appears in the New Testament with two meanings. One is the locus of redemption: "God so loved the world." The second meaning is as a symbol of darkness and opposition to God — as in "the world, the flesh, and the devil." It's in that context that John rejects (v. 17) the kind of life of the worldling who swaggers to deceive others and himself into the belief that his values — material possessions, greed — are those which matter.

John gives his list of the world's three enemies of the soul. These are carnal allurements, enticements for the eye, the life of empty show — in other words, sensual lust, covetousness, and overbearing self-confidence. They're often rendered also as "the lust of the flesh, the lust of the eyes, and the pride of life."

Carnal allurements are the inordinate desire for the pleasure of the senses. *Inordinate*, because these pleasures — be they food or drink or sex — are created by God and are good in themselves. Enticements for the eye are an inordinate desire for the world's goods — in other words, greed. The life of empty show renders John's original Greek *alazoneia.* That's the behavior of an *alazon*, a vagabond who wanders around the world living on his wits; it's the empty swagger by which he tries to deceive himself and others into the belief that he's a very fine fellow.

Luke concludes our gospel passage by telling us that the Holy Family returned to Nazareth. Pope Paul VI, in ending a visit to Nazareth, spoke (Jan. 5, 1964) of some lessons to be learned there:

"First, we learn from its silence.... The silence of Nazareth should teach us how to meditate in peace and quiet, to reflect on the deeply spiritual, and to be open to the voice of God's inner wisdom and the counsel of his true teachers. Nazareth can teach us the value of study and preparation, of meditation, of a well-ordered personal spiritual life, and of silent prayer that is known only to God.

"Second, we learn about family life. May Nazareth... show us the family's holy and enduring character and exemplifying its basic function in society: a community of love and sharing, beautiful for the problems it poses and the rewards it brings; in sum, the perfect setting for rearing children....

"Finally, in Nazareth, the home of a craftsman's son, we learn about work and the discipline it entails. I would especially like to recognize its value — demanding yet redeeming — and to give it proper respect..." (*Divine Office*, Feast of the Holy Family).

Like Anna, we're gifted with God's grace as we grow spiritually. Let her example help us reach out and spread the Good News of God's love. And as with the Holy Family in Nazareth, let's keep in mind the importance of religion to family life and of family life to society.

December 31 —
Seventh Day in the Octave of Christmas

1 Jn 2:18-21; Jn 1:1-18

Jesus our Life and our Light

Because authors must capture the attention of readers as quickly as possible, one scholar searched through the best first paragraphs he could find in famous writers. He concluded that the greatest first paragraph ever written is the beginning of St. John's gospel. This paragraph presents a great canvas of eternity and gets down to earth with the coming of Christ. For John to write like this he must have read Homer and the Book of Genesis, and John's first paragraph is bigger than both of them.

On this last day of our calendar year and next-to-last day of the end of the Octave of Christmas, it's fitting that we think about John's paragraph. Seven days after reading this passage on Christmas Day, we hear again the majestic announcement of the Incarnation. Light, life, love, healing, grace, and truth are the riches accompanying the Child born to us.

In the first words of his gospel — "In the beginning" — we see an echo of the very first words of the Bible and a contrast with "the final hour" mentioned in today's first reading. From the very beginning was the one whom John calls "the Word." "Word" in Greek (the language John wrote in) is *Logos,* which meant everything from "word" all the way to "the meaning of existence."

John was announcing that in Jesus we find the ultimate explanation of the meaning of life. He saw that the Word was in God's presence — not as a single action of the past, but in a continuous, timeless existence. But also the Word *was* God — so the Word, Jesus, is in the best position to reveal God.

Then John, like a composing artist, enunciates the two themes of his work: *life* and *light*. The life of which he speaks is the life of God: the eternal life that God lives, the opposite of destruction, condemnation, and death — and the lies of which today's first reading speaks. Life for human beings isn't mere existence — even stones exist — but a sharing in the being of God. The word *life* is frequently on the lips of Jesus. In John's gospel alone, the word *life* occurs more than 35 times, and the verb *to live* or *to have life* over 15 times more. At the very end of his gospel, John says that he has written in order that through belief in Jesus we may have life in his name (20:31).

John's *light* is the everlasting light, the timeless light revealed in time, the light that shone around the shepherds and guided the Magi. It's that light which came into God's own people, and they didn't receive it. The real light has come into the world and made its dwelling among us in and through Jesus. The word *light* occurs in John's gospel no fewer than 21 times.

Light is precious. In Jesus' time, the average home had very small windows, to prevent the loss of heat in winter and provide coolness in summer. Their homes' small lamps were like gravy boats with a lighted wick floating in oil. Their major source of light was the sun. Today, although we have lightbulbs of all shapes and sizes, all able to be turned on and off by the flick of a switch, light is still precious. And it continues to be many things: a light in the hallway soothes a frightened child, headlights point out the road, a flashlight comes to the rescue of a power blackout. Light brings warmth and love. Light also induces growth: plants and trees seek the light.

On a more humorous level, a university professor recently introduced to his class what he termed "one of the finest, most elegant lines in the English language. 'Walk with the light,'" he quoted, and then added "Now, isn't that a wonderful thing to say to someone?" The class agreed, and wanted to know the author. "I suppose it's anonymous," he said. "It's written on a sign at the intersection of Main and Ninth Streets."

Like light, our role in the world is public: discipleship can't be a merely private affair any more than light can. But spiritually we don't produce our own light: we're reflections of Jesus' light. We're like the bride who's said to be radiant: her shining radiance comes from her love.

Darkness, the antithesis of light, stands for life without Christ. One of humankind's oldest fears is fear of the dark — still present in children, and even for adults full of foreboding. Jesus is the *true* light (v. 9): different from the light given by deceptions and illusions which people have followed. Jesus the true light dissipated the darkness of doubt, of despair, of death. To those who accept Jesus and his values God gives the power to become His children (v. 12).

That brings John to the climax of his hymn: what we've been celebrating this season — the Word made flesh (v. 14). Flesh stands for all that's transitory, mortal, and at first sight seemingly incompatible with God. Yet the infinite one, the creator, the divine, became one of us, and was born in the insignificant town of Bethlehem, in a smelly stable.

At the same time as he's human, Jesus is God. All that the word "God" conveys finds adequate expression in Jesus Christ. By having lived among us, Jesus enables us to come to the heart of God. There have always been those who disbelieved, their position summed up in the ditty, "Had I been the Deity's adviser, methinks I might have planned it wiser." Deeper reflection proves the wisdom of the way God did it.

No matter how poorly this past year may have gone in our personal lives, today's gospel tells us how much has been given us in Christ, and how much can still come to pass in us. A man who had the terrible experience as a ten-year-old of finding his mother murdered wrote that over the years he had learned that "the abandonment of self-pity is the beginning of wisdom."

On this last day of the calendar year, our reading from the First Letter of St. John confronts us with the "final hour" of the antichrists. The author spoke from the perspective of his own time, when many Christians expected at any moment the end of the world and the second coming of Christ. For any number of unworthy reasons — personal gain, or insanity, or bad theology, or religious drive — certain people would claim to be the Christ or at least his representative.

There were many catastrophes at the time. The whole Church was plunged into persecution and traumatic decisions. Christians had broken with the ancestral Jewish religion to which Jesus himself had belonged. Exploding in their midst was the Roman destruction of Jerusalem in 70 A.D. The early Church was frequently swept with "end-of-the-world" movements and keen expectations of Jesus' second coming.

John's letter put these movements aside and settled down with the Church and the sacramental remembrances of Christ's presence. Rather than wait for Jesus' second coming, the Church worships the Lord mystically in the sacraments and in God's word in the Sacred Scriptures.

For us, the end of the old year and the ringing in of the new provides an opportunity to face up to our responsibilities and failures over the past three hundred and sixty-five days. Today is a good time for taking stock of the year now ending and for making resolutions for the year about to begin.

Everybody wishes others "A Happy New Year." Most people mean by that blessings like a year free from illness, pain, trouble, and worry; that everyone smile on you; that you flourish; and that the news is good every day. A good year for Christians is one in which both joys and sorrows have helped them to love God and neighbor a bit more.

On this last day of the calendar year, may we enhance our relationship with Jesus our life and our light, reveal it through our love, and thus provide for ourselves and those around us a Happy New Year and many more to come!

January 1

Nb 6:22-27; Gal 4:4-7; Lk 2:16-21

Happy New Year!

The first noun of today's gospel — shepherds — is mindful of a story. In the Fall of 1945, the Blessed Mother was said to have appeared in the Bronx (of all places!) to a nine-year-old boy named Joseph. It probably wasn't true, but the boy's situation in life gives us an idea of the level of the shepherds to whom the baby Jesus appeared.

The boy's father was a garbage collector who was an alcoholic and wife-beater. His mother, a pious woman, had 18 children, only 11 of whom survived. As he grew, young Joseph lived through years of poverty in a drafty ramshackle house. He was often out of a job, but he married and had two daughters. Among his various menial jobs, at one point he was employed at racetracks, collecting urine and blood samples from the horses. He wound up working as a janitor at a hospital.

Whether the visions were true or not, Joseph's socio-economic niche in society was about the same as that of the shepherds who found Mary and Joseph and the infant lying in the manger (v. 16) the first Christmas night. Those shepherds were looked down upon by their contemporaries, and yet they were the first, aside from Mary and Joseph, to receive the Good News. (Already we see the topsy-turviness of Christianity.)

Whereas the shepherds when they saw and understood God's message (v. 17) became active in spreading the good news far and wide (v. 18), Mary silently reflected upon the deeper meaning of the mystery (v. 19). Her reflection was a searching and a wondering as well as an acceptance. The questions flooded in: the whys, the whats, and the hows — her mysterious pregnancy, the initial distrust by Joseph, the birth in a cave-shelter for animals. All of it caused a wilderness experience — an encounter with dark isolation.

In religion, the word "loneliness" expresses the *pain* of being alone; the word "solitude" can express the *glory* of being alone. The experience of loneliness can exist for everyone — married, single, leaders, workers, the young, the old, and people in between. Religious solitude comes to few people.

Mary, like Joseph, always abided by God's law. One prescription of that law was that throughout the ages, every male among the Jews, when he is eight days old, shall be circumcised (Gn 17:12). This was a very sacred ritual: God had given circumcision to Abraham as a sign of the covenant between God and the Israelites.

At that procedure the child was also named. Today, parents choose names to retain a family tradition, or from the name of a celebrity, or simply because a certain name sounds good. In Jesus' time, the name was ordinarily suggested by the mother, but it was the father who made the final decision. The angel had told Joseph that he was to name this child Jesus, which is from the Hebrew *yoshu'a,* meaning "Yahweh has saved" or "Yahweh is salvation." Saving people was the purpose of his coming into the world, and of his life and work. So the child was named Jesus (v. 21).

Mary is an inspiration for disciples of Jesus who want to listen to his Good News. We need Mary for our spiritual lives: her tenderness, her compassion, her intuitive love. What better New Year's resolution could we make than to adopt Mary's stance before the Word-made-flesh: making her contemplative gaze our own and keeping the incarnate God before our mind and heart.

Mary is a model for us also in the way she exercised her freedom and maturity, aspects of life treasured in today's excerpt from the Letter to the Galatians. We have the freedom to receive the status of God's adopted children and enter into our inheritance. That adoption isn't by natural birth, of course, but by God's action — that is, by grace. The call to grace, ultimately, is a call to be one with God, hence a call to total adulthood in which both spiritual growth and the process of psychological maturation are inseparable.

The proof that we're literally God's children comes from the instinctive cry of our heart whereby we want to be intimate with God. This cry is to call God *Abba*, the Aramaic word for father. The sound of it is so sacred and intimate in the Letter to the Galatians that it's kept in the original tongue. The Aramaic here means "*my* father" rather than "*the* father," and has overtones in English of "daddy." It's an extremely exalted privilege that the Christian, by virtue of being God's child and thus a brother or sister of Jesus, is entitled to pray to the Father with the same intimate formula that was used by Jesus himself.

We're called to be mature, full-grown people. Growing up is the act of stepping from childhood into adulthood — actually, more of a fearful leap than a step, a leap that many people never take. To grow from the simple trust of early childhood into a personal, reflective, integrated, truly committed, and mature faith is possible for most people only after they've passed through the turmoil of adolescence.

Today's civil celebration is an occasion when people wish each other well for the year to come. The wish for a "Happy New Year" goes back to the religious notion of blessing, as in today's first reading from the Book of Numbers. A blessing recognizes that since the fall of Adam the world has contained a tension between good and evil. A blessing comprises two elements: the expulsion of Satan's power — evil — and God's taking possession.

The common Hebrew verb for "to greet" often meant "to bless." When one Jew blessed another, that blessing was considered a petition to God; when a Jew blessed God, it was an expression of praise and gratitude. The blessing in today's first reading is so beautiful that it's an integral part, not only of Jewish services, but of many Christian ones as well. It reads: "The Lord bless you and keep you! The Lord let His face shine upon you, and be gracious to you! The Lord look upon you kindly and give you peace!"

The request that the Lord let His face shine upon you is most interesting. Developmental psychology has shown that very early in life a baby shows a unique interest in faces or even shapes that resemble faces. Nature has programmed the child to engage with his or her care-givers and evoke a response from them. This process is a first stage in the child's learning to interact with others. The baby Jesus' gazing on the face of Mary taught him how to become "a man like us." The later stories that relate Jesus' ease in relating to the wealthy as well as the poor are, on a human level, rooted in this initial socialization process. God's face shining upon us raises us to new heights.

In the Christian tradition growing from the New Testament, we find many beautiful blessings. At the end of Mass, the priest always blesses God's people before sending them into the world to love and serve the Lord. And the Church's book of rituals contains blessings of water, houses, medals, lights, bread, ships, automobiles, and all kinds of other things. It is, then, uniquely fitting that we extend our heartfelt blessings for a "Happy New Year."

Let's take with us some of the lessons of today's liturgy that are a book of instructions for making a happy new year: from the first reading's Book of Numbers, to live in joy because God the Father blesses us; from the Letter to the Galatians, to live in mature freedom because His Son redeems us; and from Luke's gospel, to live reflectively under the inspiration of the Holy Spirit, like Mary.

January 2

1 Jn 2:22-28; Jn 1:19-28

Who Are You?

Of all the titles we give John — "the Baptist," or "the baptizer," "the immerser," "the dipper" — he might with equal accuracy be called "the witness." Although his witness was primarily to Jesus, today's gospel tells of his witness about himself when the "important" Jews came from Jerusalem to ask his identity (v. 19).

It was a time when, because of John's attractiveness and because some of his followers were disillusioned over Jesus' not showing all the spectacular "signs" they expected of the Messiah, they weren't becoming Christians. In fact, John's unconverted followers continued to spread throughout the whole Mediterranean world. St. Paul encountered them, still unconverted to Jesus, at Ephesus and in Asia Minor (Ac 18:24-19:4); some were also in Alexandria in Egypt.

The first question the religious authorities asked John was direct: "Who are you?" It's a question which is continually asked of us, perhaps unspoken, by others — and, hopefully, about ourselves by ourselves too, especially at times like the beginning of a new year.

John answered forthrightly, first with a negative definition of himself. Because they were looking forward to the Messiah, John answered that he wasn't he. Because they were awaiting the prophet Elijah who had been taken up to heaven and was expected — and is still awaited by religious Jews — to return to prepare the way of the Lord, John said likewise that he wasn't he. Nor was he a prophet like Moses, anticipations of whose return were also current in several circles. We, too, need to say who we're not — to have a healthy and humble sense that we aren't defined by the expectations of others, nor by our job, nor by our family, nor by our fantasies.

More positively, John quoted a text (Is 40:3) that every one of the gospels uses about him: that he was the voice of one crying out in the desert, "Make straight the way of the Lord" (v. 23). The roads of the time weren't paved, or even surfaced, unless a king or a conqueror was about to travel on them. Then repairmen would straighten the roads over which the Great One's litter would be carried.

John's answer was startling, unique, and beautiful. Our positive self-definition should, like his, also give expression to our singularity, our creativity, and our value.

The Pharisees' emissaries weren't satisfied with the Baptist's answers, and asked about his authority (v. 25). Why was he baptizing? It was a proper question. The Baptist was making believing Jews do what only unbelievers who were coming into the Jewish faith had had to do: wash to be clean enough to be one of God's people. He pointed to Christ, the one among them whom they didn't recognize (v. 26) — a remark that applies to our generation as well. John humbly observed that he wasn't worthy to untie this one's sandal-strap (v. 27). The unfastening of a master's sandals was a slave's work; the rabbis of the time had a saying that a disciple could do anything for his master but unfasten his sandals, because that job was simply too lowly.

So John the Baptist, the greatest of the prophets, is one who gave witness to Christ — the way, the truth, and the life, the way of love that casts out fear. The life of John the Baptist was such that it drew many ordinary people to repentance and even led the religious rulers of the time to wonder if he were the waited-for Messiah.

The First Letter of St. John, from which we will read for over a week more, is full of strong assertions that in Jesus God took on human flesh. That's what Christmas is all about. Perhaps, because the Christmas season closes soon, we feel sad. Today, both John the writer and John the Baptist were experiencing sadness for a different reason. Both knew that the people to whom they were writing and preaching needed to deepen their faith in Jesus. Faith is a gift, but a gift that needs to be used in order to deepen.

Both readings today anticipate the coming of the Lord. In John's letter, we're advised about when Jesus reveals himself. In the gospel, John the Baptist identified his mission as being to make ready the way of the Lord. He did that by simplicity, directness, humility, austerity, and a call to conversion.

The Baptist signals for conversion in a direct way. He was convinced of the urgency with which everyone must act. Although the First Letter of John had little patience for involved theological questions, it faces up to some of the early heresies within the Church.

It seems that Jesus must come again and again, Christmas by Christmas, new year by new year. It's always the same Lord Jesus, but always a diverse set of circumstances — to which Jesus adapts himself.

January 3

1 Jn 2:29-3:6; Jn 1:29-34

Keeping Ourselves Pure for Jesus

Once a king held a great ball to which all the people were invited. The king came disguised as a pig keeper. His pig keeper, for his part, came disguised in the king's robes. No one recognized the real king nor paid him any attention, but all fawned upon the pig keeper in the king's robes. Both reactions fitted the people's preconceived notions.

At times we have preconceived notions of Jesus. We have no trouble seeing him in the kind, the considerate, those who see eye to eye with us, and those who do what we consider proper. But what about that provokingly talkative woman who invariably sits next to us on the bus and smells in dire need of a bath? Or that asthmatic man who seems to manage always to sit behind us in church and constantly wheezes and coughs down our neck? Or the woman who lives next door who unfailingly walks her barking dog in front of where we live? Are there no limits to people in whom we're expected to see Jesus?

In the gospels' kind of "snapshot" presentations of Jesus, today the Baptist gives witness to three titles that can be given only to Jesus.

One title we might call "The Greater One": He ranks ahead of me, said John (v. 30). But for the Baptist that was hindsight, and it always troubled him that he hadn't immediately recognized Jesus. "I did not know him," John regrets (v. 31). The Baptist certainly knew that Jesus was his cousin, but he didn't know what Jesus was destined to be. Enlightenment had come at Jesus' baptism, when John saw heaven pay its tribute. And the Baptist's response in word and action at that time was the theme of his life: He must increase, I must decrease.

A second title under which the Baptist saw Jesus may be termed "The Vehicle of the Spirit" (vv. 32f.). At Jesus' baptism, the Baptist saw the Spirit come down like a dove (v. 32). The Spirit meant the Jewish *ruach*, wind, and by extension power, life, and God — especially God. The First Testament prophets had foretold an outpouring of the Spirit in the Messianic age. The New Testament sees its fulfillment in Pentecost and in baptism.

A third title for Jesus from the Baptist is "God's Chosen One" (v. 34), an allusion to Isaiah (42:1), recognizing in Jesus the special Son of God, the chosen one in whom God delights.

But all these titles, though correct, can leave us relatively cold and unresponsive. If Jesus had been presented only under these titles, he would have gradually faded from history. But then, what image might be sufficient to open up human hearts? John's answer: a young, guiltless lamb frolicking in a field, before whom children giggle and adults smile. Contrary to expectations of a Messiah of power, Jesus the Lamb took upon himself the sins of the world and died for them.

Some time ago, on a Christian mission in southern Sudan, a group of children came for instruction. The instructions began on Ash Wednesday and were to end with their baptism on Holy Saturday. On Ash Wednesday, the Maryknoll missioner gave the children a newborn lamb to be in their care. The lamb stumbled awkwardly at first, but soon playfully charged at the children, who fed it milk from a bottle.

All through Lent, the lamb grew to be more gentle and accepting, innocent, and trusting. The lamb, which always liked to be with the children, was never troublesome or demanding. When the children sat in a circle, the lamb played within it. A strong bond grew between the lamb and the children. Toward the end of Lent, the catechists explained how they would have their Holy Thursday Eucharist, which would be followed by a special community meal. And they announced that their little lamb would be the paschal lamb.

On Holy Thursday morning, there were special prayers. Then a catechist slaughtered the little lamb. They watched as even in its last moments the lamb seemed to trust them. The meal was well prepared, and the children ate the meat because meat came so seldom to their table. But there was a mood of quiet sadness — and there was tremendous awareness of Jesus the Lamb of God.

Thus the most precious of all the titles which the Baptist poignantly ascribed to the loving, lonesome Jesus is "Lamb of God" — the vulnerable lamb who dies that we might live. The Lamb of God, an image of fragility as well as whimsy and tenderness, surrenders himself to nourish us, his people, in love, in innocence, and at the cost of his life.

John the Evangelist, of course, who wrote today's gospel, sees in the figure a reference to the Passover (Paschal) lamb.

When the Jews were in Egypt and the Angel of Death was killing the firstborn of every human being and animal in Egypt, the Jews received instructions to smear the blood of a lamb on their doorposts so the angel would know them and pass over them (Ex 12:11-13). It was the blood of the lamb that protected them.

Ever after, the Passover lamb evoked images of the liberation of God's people. So sacred was the daily custom of sacrificing lambs at the Temple that the sacrifices never stopped, even in war and famine, until the Temple was destroyed by the Romans in 70 A.D. Even as the Baptist was giving witness, a Passover feast wasn't far off (Jn 2:13); at a following Passover, the lambs would be slain by the priests in the Temple at the very hour that Jesus was being put to death.

A line in today's first reading (3:3) says that everyone who has hope based on Jesus keeps himself pure, as he is pure. Do we have the generous spirit and open-mindedness of the Baptist in order that we may be happy for others to benefit from our work and even get the credit? And do we fully appreciate the Lamb of God and keep ourselves as pure as he?

January 4

1 Jn 3:7-10; Jn 1:35-42

More Witness to Christ

Jesus' first disciples John, Andrew, and Simon Peter responded to his call readily. The first time they met, John and Andrew were with the Baptist, then their teacher, at roughly the spot at the Jordan River where the Jewish people had long ago crossed into the promised land.

The Baptist, seeing Jesus go by, for the second time in two

days uttered a statement that was full of mystery and full of suggestion: "Behold ("Look!") the Lamb of God." (v. 36). "Behold" is an exclamation of revelation at key moments that causes spectators to stop and take notice. Pilate would point to the scourged Jesus and proclaim, "Behold your King!" And from the cross the dying Jesus would say of the disciple John to his mother, "Behold your son," and to John, "Behold your mother."

As yesterday's meditation showed, John the Baptist pointed to Jesus in the figure of a Lamb. Because an animal is alive as we are, yet unknown, people have sometimes used animals to express divine traits. The ancient Egyptians couldn't understand the cat — who can? — and for hundreds of years looked upon it as divine. As for the lamb, it was the usual sacrificial offering in the liturgy of the Old Covenant. That's why its image is so suggestive of the Savior, as one who surrendered himself into the hands of people, to be consumed upon the sacrificial altar.

When John and Andrew heard the names that the Baptist had attributed to the passing one — Lamb, Rabbi, Messiah — they understood enough to follow Jesus (v. 37). Like youths leaving home for the religious life, it was undoubtedly a struggle for the two to leave the Baptist. For the Baptist's part, one of his many good qualities was his complete lack of jealousy; he let them go, but he felt a great loss as he watched his disciples fade into the distance.

The two followed Jesus respectfully, a distance behind. Jesus turned and asked them what they were looking for (v. 38). This becomes a question on which discipleship hinges. John and Andrew could have been looking for almost anything. They could have been legalists, looking for exotic discussions about the Mosaic Law. They could have been opportunists looking for power. They could have been Zealots looking for allies to overthrow Rome. They could have been men of prayer looking for God's will. Or they could simply have been bewildered men looking for sympathetic guidance.

In Jesus' time, people were looking for the end of the world, or for the final battle between the forces of good and evil, or for the triumph of justice, or for the final victory of God. People still come to Jesus looking for a variety of things: a security blanket, or an escape from problems, or an insurance policy for life hereafter, or a prescription to enable them to live without bother, or for many other things.

John and Andrew began their answer with the most complimentary title they could think of: "Rabbi" — Teacher. This was even though John had told them that he is much more than this. Andrew explained to his brother Simon that "we've found the Messiah." However wonderful, the assertion falls short of the full recognition of Jesus which the reader today knows from John's Prologue to his gospel.

The title "rabbi" in this case wasn't mere flattery. They followed it by asking where Jesus stayed. They wanted more than a superficial relationship. Jesus' answer was a kind invitation to come and see for themselves (v. 39). The invitation wasn't only to *talk*, but to *hear* what he could reveal to them; not only to *look at* something, but to *look into* it. They accepted. Jesus took them to the place where he was living — perhaps a cave — and they stayed with him that day.

The occasion was so memorable to John the Evangelist that he even adds the time of day at which he met Jesus: four in the afternoon. Indeed, John's association with Jesus affected the Evangelist so deeply that it would color everything he wrote. John would disclose the nerve-center of Jesus' life to be prayer: communion and intimacy with his heavenly Father. He would write that through Jesus we know what God is like and what people can become.

Simon Peter's brother Andrew (v. 40), is a most attractive character. For one thing, he was always content to play second fiddle to Peter. For another, he simply couldn't keep good news to himself. The New Testament mentions him only three times, each time seeming to delight in introducing people to Jesus. In one (Jn 6:8f.), he brought to Jesus the boy with the five loaves and two fish to be multiplied for thousands of people. In another (Jn 12:22), he and Philip brought inquiring people of culture to Jesus.

In today's passage, the first thing Andrew did was seek out his brother Simon and bring him to meet Jesus (vv. 40f.). And what a meeting that was! The Evangelist records that Jesus *looked at* Simon (v. 42) — that special, intense, concentrated look of love that sees not only what's on the surface, but inner depths. That special look no one ever forgot. For once in his life Simon seemed too overwhelmed to make any remarks.

Andrew would be crucified for Christ on an X-shaped cross. That was the origin of the use of an X to signify a kiss. It began when the majority of people were illiterate and unable to even sign their own name. Having to testify to documents, they put an X in place of a signature. Without it a contract was considered invalid. To affirm their sincerity, they solemnly kissed the X, in the same way that they used to kiss the Bible when taking an oath. Eventually the kiss and the X became synonymous. The choice of the X, the sign of St. Andrew, implied a sacred guarantee and promise to fulfill one's obligation.

As for Simon, Jesus changed his name to Peter. In the ancient world, almost everybody had at least two names. One was in his native language, by which he was known to his family and close friends. The other was in Greek, the language of culture and commerce, by which he was known in the business world. For the ancient Israelites, a change of name often denoted a change of relationship with God: the person was considered to be getting a fresh start.

What insight and vision it took to change Simon's name to Peter! The word (*Petrus* in Latin, *Petros* in Greek) meant Rock, with all its connotations of solidity and stability — qualities which, in the beginning at least, no one who knew Peter (except

Jesus) could possibly attribute to him. But when God looks at us He sees not only what we are, but also what we can become.

In the first reading for today — this early day in the beginning of the year — St. John tells us that the devil is a sinner from the beginning. "Beginning," particularly in the writings of John, generally reaches back to the timelessness of eternity, where the "Word" dwelt with God the Father (Jn 1:1). We're impressed at how carefully God was preparing for the ultimate fulfillment of prophecy and of His own eternal plans. The reading ends (v. 10) with the way that Jesus summed up his own teaching: to love one's brother and sister. Not a bad ending — or beginning!

January 5

1 Jn 3:11-21; Jn 1:43-51

True Love

A college professor had his sociology class go into the Baltimore slums to get case histories of 200 young boys. They were asked to write an evaluation of each boy's future. In every case, the students wrote, "He doesn't have a chance." Twenty-five years later another sociology professor came across the earlier study. He had his students follow up on the project to see what had happened to those boys. With the exception of 20 boys who had moved away or died, the students learned that 176 of the remaining 180 had achieved more than ordinary success as lawyers, doctors, and businessmen.

The astounded professor decided to pursue the matter further. Fortunately, all the men were still in the area, and he was able to ask each, "How do you account for your success?" In each case the reply came with feeling, "There was a teacher."

The teacher was still alive, so he sought her out and asked the old but still alert lady what magic formula she had used. Her eyes sparkled and her lips broke into a gentle smile. "It's really very simple," she said. "I loved those boys."

Both of today's readings encourage us to love — to love God and, in Him, others. Experience shows how easily selfishness wants to replace love. Our willingness to love others, to serve the good of others, requires nourishment from the teaching and the bread of Christ.

In today's gospel, when Philip introduced Nathanael to Jesus, Nathanael — reflecting the contemporary disdain for Nazareth — asked if anything good could come from there. Jesus asserted that Nathanael, unlike the deceitful Israelite patriarch Jacob, was an Israelite without guile (v. 47). The fig tree (v. 48) may be a symbol of messianic peace and plenty; it's also compared to the Law of Moses. In any case, for Nathanael it reveals Jesus' intimate knowledge of him.

Jesus said Nathanael would see the sky opened and the angels of God ascending and descending on him — in other words, a new interchange between heaven and earth. The image comes from the account of the patriarch Jacob (Gn 28:10-17). He was fearful for his life because of his twin brother Esau's jealous hatred of him and because of the hazards of his exiled living in a strange country. Through the vision of a stairway between heaven and earth, God had assured Jacob of divine protection and of blessings beyond his imagination.

Today's reading from St. John's First Letter tells us that we're to love in deed and in truth, and not merely in talk. Love has as many meanings as there are people who experience it. The dictionary says many things about love: that it's a feeling of strong personal attachment induced by ties of kinship, ardent affection, strong liking, fondness, good will, and tender and passionate affection.

Some people express love with hugs. Someone said, "Hugging is healthy. It helps maintain the body's immune system. It helps depression. It reduces stress. It's invigorating. It's rejuvenating. It has no unpleasant side effects, and hugging is nothing less than a miracle drug. Hugging is practically perfect. There are no movable parts, no batteries to wear out, low energy consumption, high energy yield, non-fattening, non-taxable and, of course, fully returnable."

You can give without loving but you can't love without giving. Love makes lovers want to give their time, energy, solace, and understanding. Love makes the lover feel warm, happy, peaceful, and content.

It's not simply hatred which is opposed to love, but — worse — indifference. Loving means seeing brothers and sisters in our neighbor — under God's fatherhood — and taking care of our neighbor's needs. Loving others enables us to "pass from death to life."

Jacob Riis was a social reformer who shocked the conscience of the United States in 1890 by descriptions of slum conditions. His lectures often ended with the words, "The first, the all-important task is to *find your neighbor*." He believed that neighboring wasn't just a matter of proximity, helping people who live next door, but an ethical charge that extended well beyond the limits of local geography. Representing the opposite of that, John's letter mentions Cain who killed his brother Abel.

Why are wicked people so actively opposed to good ones? In large part, because they perceive that the life and words of good people are a reproach to their way of living. Their proximate motives can be many: prejudice, self-interest, jealousy, hatred.

Why take the trouble to cultivate self-sacrificing love when it's possibly more fun and more glamorous to stray from the straight and narrow? For many reasons. For one, because that's the only way to preserve our self-respect, and without that our life will be miserable. Our "self" will be restless until we follow an upright conscience that tells us to love. Also, it's better to imitate the saints than to follow losers; God vividly speaks to us through them because they show His divine presence. In addition, our love should be self-sacrificing because the Kingdom is not only in the future; it begins here and now. To be fully human, we needn't be beautiful, or rich, or successful, but we do have to be loving.

Also, we're to sacrifice ourselves to love because the stakes are so high if we don't. And we're to do it because self-sacrificing love shines its own beautiful light: we want to love because it's our destiny to be one forever with the All-Loving One Himself. Lastly, there's always the contagiousness of loving. To love every man and woman as brother and sister releases within us extraordinary energy and exceptional insight. Such love summons us to new greatness.

With that kind of love, like Nathanael we will see angels ascending and descending. Like Jacob we will be strengthened for difficult actions and blessed beyond our merit. We will gain perceptions of hidden goodness in others and intuit them in ourselves, and Jesus will be whispering, "I saw you under the fig tree" — that is, I was with you as you dreamed good deeds and nourished enchanting hopes for others!

Pope John Paul II traveled many miles and visited many countries. In O'Higgins Park, in Santiago, Chile, he was presiding at a Mass of reconciliation, but it turned into a Mass of the guerillas. From the start, the guerillas fired on the tents. Then they knocked down the journalists' platform. The police arrived in armored cars. The Pope saw the stretchers going by with the bleeding wounded. At times, gusts of tear gas reached the altar. Looking over the scene, the Pope shouted, "Love is stronger."

It would be good to remember the story of the anonymous good man who said concerning his prayer: "I asked God to take away my pain. God said, 'No. It's not for me to take away, but for you to give it up.' I asked God to make my handicapped child whole. God said, 'No. Her spirit is whole, her body only temporary.' I asked God to grant me patience. God said, 'No. Patience is a by-product of tribulations; it isn't granted, it's earned.' I asked God to give me happiness. God said, 'No. I give you blessings. Happiness is up to you.' I asked God to spare me pain. God said, 'No. Suffering draws you apart from worldly cares and brings you closer to me.' I asked God to make my spirit grow. God said, 'No. You must grow on your own, but I will prune you to make you fruitful.' I asked for all things that I might enjoy life. God said, 'No. I will give you life so that you may enjoy all things.' I asked God to help me love others, as much as He loves me. God said '...Aaahh, finally you have the idea.'"

January 6

1 Jn 5:5-13; Mk 1:7-11

God's Successive Revelations about Jesus: Baptism

On the feast of Epiphany, when we commemorate the arrival of the Magi to the child Jesus, the leader of a women's Bible study group asked, "Would it have made a difference if Three Wise Women, instead of Three Wise Men, had come on the first Christmas?"

Another woman answered, "Absolutely! They would have asked for directions, arrived on time, helped deliver the baby, cleaned the stable, made a casserole, and brought disposable diapers as gifts."

Actually, the Magi's gifts were, as said in Arabic, *ilm al-djamal* — "all that is beautiful to the senses." In the ancient

Middle East, beauty was as important as air. Beauty was in the gardens that the people designed, the houses they built, the words they wrote, the bowls they used, the candlesticks they made, the fabrics they wove, and the gifts they gave.

As we contemplate the wonderful revelation of God to humankind through the Magi who came to the infant Jesus, there's no reason to think that they were especially rich. They had enough money to travel, of course, which was particularly expensive in the days when journeys would take months. Selling gold or precious substances along the way was probably the only way to gain foreign currency in the days before traveler's checks, cash machines, and credit cards.

Considering the difficulties of travel, we can imagine the Magi as being young, with a wanderlust and free of family commitments, content to sleep always in a different bed (or none). They traveled by night — how else would they be able to follow the star? — and slept by day.

The precious gifts of gold and fragrant frankincense and myrrh weren't unusual for that time and place. The gold, a fitting kingly offering, in today's market would be worth about $325 per ounce. Scents were believed to bring good will and good wishes. Frankincense and myrrh were used to perfume ceremonial oils. When burned, the smoke was thought to bring prayers to the heavens.

The Bible has many references to frankincense and myrrh resins, which were cultivated from desert-growing trees. Oils scented with them are mentioned almost 200 times. The starting point for the fragrant frankincense trail took the gums from what are now Oman, Yemen, and Somalia, and sent them up the Red Sea to Egypt and the reaches of the Roman Empire. The gums that bubble from the trees into pearly white beads can still be found in southern Oman. Oman frankincense, top grade and costly, accounts for about 10 percent of the 600 tons that are harvested worldwide every year.

The Greek historian Herodotus wrote that more than two tons were burned annually in the Temple of Baal in Babylon. Darius, King of Persia (now Iran), received some 25 tons of incense every year. The Roman emperor Nero was a great lover of the scent and burned a year's worth of the crop at the funeral of his wife, Poppea.

The Egyptians embalmed their kings with frankincense and considered the fruit of the *Boswellia* or frankincense tree the perfume of the gods that, when collected and preserved correctly, ensured immortality. The Roman historian Pliny noted in the first century A.D. how control of the frankincense trade had made the southern Arabians the richest people in the world.

However, in today's liturgy our focus is changing from the Christmas baby Jesus to the adult Jesus. We commemorate Jesus' baptism, which was the moment when he passed from the relative obscurity of village life in Nazareth onto the public stage of his mission of proclaiming God's kingdom.

Why was Jesus baptized? Baptism is meant as an acknowledgment of sin, and Jesus was sinless; as an expression of repentance, and Jesus didn't have to repent; and as the way we become children of God, and Jesus was already God's Son. Was Jesus' being baptized — even though with the non-sacramental baptism of John — much like sham play-acting?

The Baptist was reluctant to perform it. He had preached about one mightier than himself whose sandals he wasn't worthy to loose (v. 7); he recognized that whereas the baptism to be established by Jesus would be a sacramental one with the Holy Spirit (v. 8), the baptism he himself performed was only a symbolic one.

Why, then, did Jesus *want* to be baptized? For many reasons.

For one, his baptism brings about his solidarity with all the human race in our sinful condition. In the dark days when Nazism spread across much of Europe, Hitler ordered the king of Denmark to issue a decree for all the Jews in his country to publicly identify themselves by wearing a yellow armband with the Star of David on it. The king knew that anyone so identified would be sent to a death camp. He also knew the danger of disobeying Hitler's orders. So when he issued his decree, he wore a yellow armband with a Star of David on it, although he wasn't Jewish. The next day, everyone in the country — Jew and Gentile alike — wore the required armband. Solidarity with the condemned resulted in life for all.

Another reason for Jesus' being baptized is on a more natural and human plane. Up to this time, no Jew had ever wanted to submit to baptism, even a ritualistic one like John's. That was because the Jews considered themselves to be children of Abraham and by that fact assured of salvation. When people wanted to become converts to Judaism, they were considered to need purification — because the Gentiles were tainted by sin and had to be washed clean.

At this time, though, John had begun a startling movement of Jewish acknowledgment of sin and of repentance for it. The size of the crowds coming out into the desert to John showed that the Jews, as perhaps at no other time in history for them or any other people, were searching for God. Jesus saw this movement, and was happy to undergo John's baptism to signify that he identified with it (v. 9). One of the good things about that was the nature of the identification. It's easy for one to identify with a movement that's for one's benefit: a prosperous social club, for example, or a popular political movement. But it's far better when one identifies with a cause that's beyond oneself and benefits others more than oneself.

Then, too, through Jesus' baptism the early Church could argue against the followers of the Baptist who hadn't converted to Christ: that the Spirit descended upon Jesus, not John, and the approving heavenly voice spoke of Jesus, not John. The Baptist's followers could now unmistakably recognize that Jesus was the one whom God had sent. Indeed, Jesus' baptism turned out to be a moment when God showed His approval of him (vv. 10f.). In St. Mark's gospel, the descent of the Spirit and the voice from the heavens were inner experiences of Jesus which he publicly shared.

The voice of the heavenly Father was almost verbatim a quotation from Isaiah. The gospel expression "beloved son" (v. 11) means the same as Isaiah's "chosen one" (Is 42:1). When the voice came, it came from heavens that were *rent*, a central word drawn from Isaiah. That meant that the heavens were *ripped apart* — not simply "opened" — to indicate the great cataclysm that was taking place at this baptism. In Isaiah's time the people had been praying intensely, almost in desperation, that God look down from heaven. They shouted at the distant, cloudless expanse of the near eastern skies, "Oh, that you would rend those heavens and come down…" (Is 63:19).

John the Baptist couldn't hold back, the heavenly Father could remain silent no longer, the heavens would be rent — this is one of the greatest introductions of anyone in the Bible.

Those are among the reasons why Jesus was baptized. Now, why are *we* baptized? Through our baptism we receive the Spirit of adoption which makes us children of God, a second birth that's an ongoing transformation of our first. Our baptism incorporates us, in a special way, into Jesus.

Has our second birth brought a realization that we have the potential for transformation? Such a transformation means conversion. And conversion means a new vision. And a new vision of what's possible in Jesus begets mission. And mission means a search for Jesus' values, a perhaps painful awareness of the gap between our *proclaimed* values and our *lived* values.

The waters coming from the rock at Moses' command in the desert saved, but the waters of the flood brought death. The waters of baptism don't save automatically. Would our heavenly Father be able to say of each of us, as He did of Jesus, "You are my beloved child; with you I am well pleased"?

January 7

1 Jn 5:14-21; Jn 2:1-12

The Ministry Begins

In the gospels we see events on many different levels of depth and meaning. The first is the facts level, which in today's gospel is easy. Jesus, his mother, and five of his disciples were at a wedding in the little town of Cana. In a place and time of hardship and poverty, everyone in town looked forward to a wedding as one of the relieving joys of life. A wedding would take place in the evening after a feast. By that time it would be dark and, with a canopy over their heads, the newly-married couple would be conducted through the village streets in the light of torches to their new home. They would be taken by the longest route, to be seen and wished well by as many people as possible. They couldn't manage a honeymoon, so they would stay at home and for a week they held open house.

On a deeper level, Judaism saw in the joy of the wedding feast a figure of the Messianic age. Wine was, then as now, a bond of friendship when used in moderation to rejoice the heart of people. To run out of wine at a wedding was more of a humiliation for the couple than it would be today. For one thing, hospitality in the East was a sacred duty; for another, running out of wine would show poor planning, or — worse — the couple's lack of prosperity, which would mean the absence of God's blessing.

By arriving at the wedding celebration at Cana with an uninvited band of fishermen in tow, Jesus may have contributed to the wine shortage. Some cynics have humorously commented that Mary's pointing out that they had no wine (v. 3) was really saying, "The wine's finished — let's go home." More seriously, her observation wasn't a request exactly, but a mother's indirect expression of caring.

Jesus' answer began with a word that our idiom may sometimes consider discourteous: "Woman" (v. 4). On a deeper level, that word looks back to Genesis (3:15), which said that God would put enmity between Satan and "the woman," and the salutation looks forward to Jesus' words to his mother from the cross about John that she was to behold her son (Jn 19:26). In each case, it was the same message: a declaration of spiritual relationship.

Continuing on a deep level, Jesus added something he mentioned frequently: "My hour has not yet come." God's revelation in Jesus' life would reach its fullness at Our Lord's "hour," the time of his passion and death. When Jesus spoke about his "hour" here, he's saying, "Look, mother, I'll do the miracle of the transformation of the water into wine, but, mother, you who have a docile heart, look in the direction of 'my hour.'"

Mary, knowing she hadn't been repulsed, told the waiters to do whatever he told them (v. 5). At the Annunciation, Mary had wanted everything done according to the word of the Lord. In a remarkable dramatic oratorio (John Adams' *El Niño*), as the angel Gabriel approaches Mary at the Annunciation a soft rattling sound in the orchestra grows insistently louder, and isolated plucks on the strings create unease. Suddenly, a burst of searing brass and clanking chimes seems to go off inside the listener's head. Finally, this awesome mass of sound explodes. Then, over a gently rocking rhythmic figuration in the harps and strings, singers in exotic yet calming parallel harmonies tell a stupefied Mary that she will conceive "a child of might." Here at Cana Mary didn't know what Jesus would do, but she believed in him, and — unlike many of us — could trust even when she didn't understand.

The water jars were there because Jewish custom demanded many washings. These were practical for sandal-clad feet tracking in dust and dirt from unsurfaced roads. There were also ceremonial hand washings before, during, and after eating. The jars were stone because stone couldn't contract ritual uncleanness. Altogether they contained approximately 120 gallons.

At Jesus' order, the waiters filled the water jars to the brim (v. 7). On the ordinary level, this would prove that nothing but water was in them. On a deeper level, there are many meanings. The jars are as with everyone's life: to the extent that we put in, we profit. We measure life not by the number of breaths we take, but by the moments that take our breath away; we're to be *alive* while we're alive.

Then, too, the water changed into wine meant a lot of wine — but, on a deeper level, the amount of wine suggests the lavish generosity of God's grace. And the metamorphosis mirrored the Genesis story of creation, in which God's word sufficed to bring about newness.

For Jesus, this was the beginning of his signs (v. 11). Whereas the other gospels call such wondrous events miracles, St. John the Evangelist calls them signs because they point to who Jesus really is: they're sign-ificant. There's more to Jesus than meets the eye. In him, the new covenant is at hand, and it's superior to the old: the wine kept till last proves best. The Feast of the Epiphany commemorates the showing of Jesus to the Magi, and the feast of his Baptism a further showing, when the Father proclaimed Jesus as His Son. Now, at Cana, Jesus himself manifested his glory.

While the miracle may have had other motives, such as regard for his mother, kindness to his host, caring for people, approval of happy occasions, or insinuation of the Eucharist, the Evangelist implies that the first motive here was the confirmation of the incipient faith of the disciples: his disciples began to believe in him. And the transformation of the disciples into believers may be the deepest part.

The first reading is from the First Letter of John. Throughout the letter we sense the preoccupation of the Church with true doctrine and the Church's concern to center faith in the person of Jesus. We're prompted to examine our loyalty of faith and discipline: do we identify Church with the person of Jesus?

On a very deep level, we can apply today's lessons to the wedding party that is our life because Jesus wanted us to enjoy ourselves and be happy. He wasn't a killjoy: he made people feel good, like being bathed in sunshine. The people who crucified Jesus never accused him of being a bore. To the contrary, they thought him too dynamic to be safe. And later generations suffused Jesus' personality with an atmosphere of tedium and recommended him as a fitting household pet for people who were insecure, vulnerable, and retiring.

Like the party at Cana, the party of our life entails work that's serious. We should work for justice, because without justice there can be no party. We should feed the hungry, because without feeding the hungry there can be no party. We should respond to God's invitations to the ongoing love that's like that of a bride and groom, or there can be no party.

Monday after Epiphany or January 7

1 Jn 3:22-4:6; Mt 4:12-17, 23-25

Jesus' Message in Earnest

Wise people generally put great importance on beginnings. They've coined such aphorisms as "well begun is half done," "the end depends upon the beginning," and "mighty things from small beginnings grow."

Today's gospel marks some of the beginning of "the dawning of the ages." In a mere few lines, St. Matthew points out some of its signs: the arrest of John the Baptist (v. 12) signals the beginning of the New Testament; Jesus' preaching in Galilee and centering his work from Capernaum (v. 13) presents him as the light of the nations (v. 16); and the first healings by Jesus (v. 23) reveal the efficaciousness of the salvation he brings.

Galilee, where Jesus started, didn't seem a likely place for any mission to begin. The most ignorant, crass, and pagan areas of the country were the territories of Zebulun and Naphtali, where Galilee was. Matthew shared with other devout Jews the concept of Galilee as a land of darkness (vv. 15f.). And it was (in part) heathen Gentile territory, thus emphasizing — without Jesus' followers knowing it — the non-exclusive nature of his call.

The mention of place names (vv. 24f.) — Syria, Galilee, Decapolis, Jerusalem, Judea, and Transjordania — draws attention to the historical circumstances of Jesus' ministry: Christian faith isn't a body of abstract principles, but a faith based on persons, events, and places.

Geographically, Galilee was important. The great roads of the area passed through it. Because of its fertility, it was densely populated. Better still, its people were open to ideas, so that Galilee could not, like Judea, keep new concepts out. If there was any place suitable for an unprecedented teacher with a novel message, Galilee was it.

For the evangelist Matthew, the choice of Galilee went deeper. For him it was to the people of Galilee that Isaiah had announced the Messianic light. If the people of the time had read the scriptures carefully, they would have found Isaiah speaking of the people in darkness who would see a great light — a light of good coming from Zebulun and Naphtali.

Galilee had been the first part of Israel to experience the destroying wrath of Yahweh, which was through the Assyrians in 734 B.C., roughly Isaiah's time of writing. At that time the Assyrian ruler, Tiglath-Pilesar III, with his ruthlessness as a totalitarian despot, deported the local population and dispersed them throughout his expanding empire, giving birth to the fable of the "lost tribes of Israel." Isaiah held out hope for a future restoration of "the people who walked in darkness." In Matthew's view, Jesus was the fulfillment of the prophetic words of Isaiah, and Galilee the first to hear of Yahweh's salvation.

The sparkling pear-shaped Lake of Galilee had a lovely shoreline thick with fishing boats and prosperous towns. The town of Tiberias attracted tourists from the whole Greco-Roman world; it had more in common with the resorts of the Costa Brava or the Riviera today than with a sleepy fishing village in, say, Maine. This didn't help the local people's morals.

That Jesus left Nazareth and went to live in Capernaum by the Lake of Galilee (v. 13) expressed a note of finality: Jesus left his home, never to live there again. Capernaum's position was ideal for reaching a larger audience. Situated on the high road from Jerusalem in the south to Damascus in the north and serving as the frontier post of Palestine, it was a center of attraction for both Jews and foreigners.

There Jesus could preach with effectiveness. His proclamation that the people repent because the kingdom of heaven was at hand (v. 17) announced a new intervention of God. Jesus branched out into all of Galilee, teaching in their synagogues, proclaiming the gospel, and curing the people (v. 23). His fame spread to all of neighboring Syria (v. 24), and great crowds from all over followed him (v. 25). He was asking for conversion and transformation of life. That includes actively doing good works and passively being penitent, both of them toward receiving God's mercy for sins.

The insights of today's first reading, from the First Letter of St. John, shows Jesus' message in earnest. It gives a summary of the commandments in typical Johannine form. That we believe in Jesus and love one another (v. 23) may be John's version of Jesus' double command of love. In John's tradition, "to believe" in the Son whom the Father has sent is equivalent to loving God. The virtue of charity (even to the point of giving up one's life for one's neighbor as Jesus did) is the fulfillment of the commandments (v. 22ff.), the guarantee of union with God through the presence of the Holy Spirit (v. 24).

But, in matters of spiritual phenomena, delusion and deception are invariably possible (1 Jn 4:1-6). The famous Dr. Seuss (Theodore Geisel), author of such stories as *The Cat in the Hat* and *Green Eggs and Ham*, said, in a commencement address:

"My uncle ordered popovers from the restaurant's bill of fare. / When they were served he regarded them with a penetrating stare. / Then he spoke great words of wisdom, as he sat there on that chair: / 'To eat these things,' said my uncle, 'you must exercise great care. / You may swallow down what's solid — but you must spit out the air.'"

As you partake in the world's bill of fare, Seuss concluded, be careful what you swallow, and do a lot of spitting out of the hot air.

Discernment between a true and false spirit of prophecy depends on acceptance or rejection of sound doctrine. Thus, acknowledgment or denial of the central truth of Christianity, the incarnation of Jesus the Son of God, is proof of whether one belongs to God or to the Antichrist (vv. 1ff.). A power greater than that of the world abides in those who belong to God and who heed the teaching of the Apostles. Proper discernment conquers the false prophets (v. 4) who belong to the world, speak its language, and receive its attention.

Opposition between the Spirit of truth and the spirit of error reflects the opposition between the Spirit of truth and the "prince of this world" in St. John's gospel (16:11). John's gospel places a sharp division between those who "know God" and the "world" under Satan, which hears only what belongs to it.

Today's readings are intended to stir us to action. Because people who practice religion, like others, sometimes seek more their own desire for comfort and security than trying to eradicate strife and injustice, our non-religious brethren criticize practitioners of religion as being a dangerous source of further disunity and suffering. We who practice our religion should walk, as the greatest people of old walked, with our whole being flooded with joyous light.

Light acquires a transcendental quality. This goes beyond even the light of the bright Mediterranean known to the sacred writers; it's something more, something unfathomable, something holy. This is the light that penetrates directly to the soul, opens the doors and windows of the heart, and makes one effusive and radiant. Let's pray that we may be the light of one small candle that may ignite a thousand. Well begun is half done, and mighty things from small beginnings grow.

Tuesday after Epiphany or January 8

1 Jn 4:7-10; Mk 6:34-44

Spiritual Nourishment

Sharing food with people isn't as simple as it sounds. Ask any political candidate in the United States who has followed the campaign ritual, eating his way caterpillar-like through ethnic neighborhoods: the kosher hot dog, the Irish soda bread, the Italian cannoli, the German wurst, the Polish kielbasa. Politicians have found food to be tribal bonding: I eat what you eat; so we have something in common; so vote for me.

So important to *spiritual* nourishment is Jesus' multiplication of food in today's gospel that it's the only one of Jesus' miracles told by all four evangelists. The opening line proclaims how godlike were the human emotions of Jesus: he saw a great crowd and his heart was moved to pity for them. The miracle is meant to be a tribute to Jesus' compassion rather than a manifestation of his power.

As for his compassion, although he had taken the Apostles away from the crowd for a well-deserved rest, when over 5,000 men, not counting women and children, came to see him he not only tolerated their disturbing his plans but, in contrast with the abhorrence of the Twelve who wanted to dismiss the people, he actively welcomed them. While Jesus was acting on the level of compassion, his disciples were reacting on the level of practicality. You can get some idea of his kind of compassion if you imagine your reaction to your hard-earned vacation being disturbed by a crowd of acquaintances, hangers-on, or unknowns coming to your vacation retreat to freeload.

Social divisions were more pronounced in Jesus' time than in ours — and yet it would seem that he made sharing food on an equal footing one of the key points of his way of relating to the world of his time. Just think of the groupings who were fighting each other who might have been present in the people who were now sitting down together. Men and women of the time would normally not have eaten together, nor would those Jews who were ritually pure with those who were unclean. There was also the separation of Jews and Gentiles, not to mention peasants and those of a higher social order.

Jesus' banquet of love contrasted with another banquet that immediately preceded it: the self-indulgent banquet of Herod Antipas. At Herod's banquet there was pride, arrogance, scheming, and the murder of John the Baptist; at Jesus' banquet there's love, understanding, healing, trust, and sharing.

Besides Jesus' satisfying the hunger of the people, especially worthy of note is also the *abundance* of God's generosity. God's generosity is a recurring theme throughout the Bible. God had given in abundance the manna which He had freely provided to the hungry Hebrews as they wandered through the vast and trackless desert in their exodus from Egypt. Jesus' life reflected the heavenly Father's generosity in the lavishness of the wine at Cana, the copious water which he promised the Samaritan woman at the well, and the plenitude of the Spirit which he promised would be poured out. Here, it showed for individuals: each person ate, everybody had more than enough, and there was sufficient left over to fill twelve baskets.

The gospel's account of Jesus' taking the bread, giving thanks, and distributing it, all refer forward to the Eucharist. The same God who could perform this miracle could do anything, including changing bread and wine into his body and blood. The Eucharist is a special kind of food: one which we need as much for the nourishment of our spiritual life as we need material food for our bodily life. The Eucharist makes us companions — from the Latin *cum* and *panis,* literally "bread-sharers" — with God and each other. To those who use the eucharistic bread properly, Jesus offers the same compassion and the same abundance of results as he did in today's gospel.

The first reading is like a commentary on the effulgent love manifested by Jesus in his emotions, which he expected of his disciples. Since love is God's own nature, we're exhorted to love in turn. We often say that love is blind; but most of us, most of the time, are blind to love. But anyone who knows that he or she has been truly loved has been transformed by that experience. For them, life is different.

This passage puts it succinctly in saying that true love consists in God loving us and sending His Son as an offering for our sins. In comparison, our love isn't much. God has loved us *first* — freely, spontaneously, compassionately. God's revelation of His love consisted in His sending His Son into our world as our Savior, in order that we might have life through him. We haven't merited Jesus' love, and Jesus' love continues the love which is in God. In the mercy and forgiveness of Jesus' death we have the motive for our love for one another.

The grandeur of God's love is like the expanse of the sky, the height of mountains, and the depth of the sea, all of which defy our normal instruments for measuring. We can do no less than use the spiritual nourishment He has given us to respond in kind.

Wednesday after Epiphany or January 9

1 Jn 4:11-18; Mk 6:45-52

Be Open to Growth — Especially in Faith and Love

After Jesus' miracle of the multiplication of the loaves and fish, the Apostles seemed to like the peoples' idea of making Jesus their king. In today's gospel, which follows immediately upon the miracle, St. Mark tells us that Jesus *insisted* that his disciples get into the boat and that he actively had to *dismiss* the crowds. Had they foreseen Jesus' departure, the most unruly spirits in the crowd would have laid hold of all the available boats and followed.

The people's fascination wasn't because of God's revealing a facet of himself, but a much more mundane desire for magic and an ongoing free fast-food meal ticket. The obvious manifestation of power in multiplying bread and fish they perceived at once. The compassionate love of God in Jesus for sheep without a shepherd eluded them.

Jesus, in this moment of achievement, went up on the mountain alone to pray. The gospels often mention Jesus praying alone the night before important events. This time, it was to acknowledge that the heavenly Father was the source of his power, and because the next day he would talk about the Eucharist.

The Apostles rowed away from the scene across the Lake of Galilee. At about three o'clock in the morning, hard-pressed by having to row against strong head winds in their little boat, they saw something walking toward them on the water. The storm was threatening to destroy them just when they were at the very thing they know best — handling a boat. Engrossed in their difficulties, they were unable to discern the coming of Jesus.

"The thing" out there seemed to have a human shape, so all they could think of was a ghost. They were more terrified of ghosts than of the accustomed heavy winds and high waves. Their shouts weren't merely out of terror, but — in accord with the superstition of their time — they thought that shouting was the way you got rid of ghosts. A humorous church sign read: "The sermon this morning: 'Jesus Walks on the Water.' The sermon tonight: 'Searching for Jesus.'"

Strangely, whereas the presence of Jesus should mean peace, it was the presence of Jesus that made them fearful! An artist was commissioned by a wealthy man to paint something that would depict peace. After a great deal of thought, he painted a beautiful country scene: green fields with cows, birds in a blue sky, and a lovely little village in a distant valley. When the artist presented the painting, there was a look of disappointment on the sponsor's face. He said to the artist, "There's something that just isn't right. Could you try again?"

The artist went back to his studio, thought for several hours about peace, then went to his canvas to paint. When he was finished, on his canvas was a mother holding a sleeping baby in her arms, smiling lovingly at her child. He hurried to present this painting to his sponsor. But again his sponsor asked the artist to try again.

The painter returned to his studio — discouraged, tired, disappointed, and angry at the rejection. Now he prayed for inspiration to do a painting of true peace. All of a sudden, an idea came, and he began to paint as he had never painted before. When he finished, he hurried to present his painting to his sponsor.

As the artist held his breath, his sponsor studied the painting carefully for several minutes. Finally the sponsor said, "Now this is a picture of true peace." He accepted the painting, paid the artist, and both artist and sponsor were happy.

What was this painting of true peace? The artist had captured the fury of the wind as it whipped about in the darkness in a pounding, stormy sea. The sea was roaring, waves churning, the dark sky filled with the power of ferocious thunder and lightning. And in the middle of the picture, under the gunwales of a boat, the artist had painted a small bird, safe and dry, snuggled in her nest. The bird was at peace amidst the storm that raged around her.

Often, like the Apostles, we're afraid to step out of secure positions. Preconceived ideas take over, fear overcomes our faith, and we remain safely inside ourselves. It would be better to leave ourselves open — truly and completely open, without preconceived ideas — to God's way of being and doing in our lives and in our world.

St. John shows us the way to do that in today's first reading, one of the jewels of the New Testament. Because John was an old man when he wrote, he spoke of those things which he considered the most important. He wrote on his favorite theme, the virtue that fascinated him most, the virtue which shows that we belong to Jesus: love.

John repeats the most inexhaustible statement in scripture (v. 16): "God is love." God's love surrounds us like the air we breathe. John reminds us that the one who abides in love abides in God, and God in that person. Yet all of us can testify how difficult love can be. Most people, it seems, would prefer to *discuss* love rather than to *practice* it.

John shows that the means by which we know God's love is Jesus. God's love sent Jesus as a person with heart — a heart that humanly rejoiced, had pity, and suffered. We're to exercise some measure of the same kind of love. John indicates the paradox that it's only by knowing God that we learn to love, and only by loving that we come to know God.

But, as John implies, a more abiding constant in life seems to be fear. The history of the Incarnation opens with the words, "Don't be afraid, Mary" (Lk 1:30). The angel of the Lord gave the same admonition to Joseph (Mt 1:20). And to the shepherds in the Christmas fields the angels repeated, "Don't be afraid" (Lk 2:10). As John says here, though, there's no fear in love. In the worst times of the murderous Pinochet regime in Chile, a nun was on her way to see a high-ranking general to defend a poor neighbor whose son was being detained by the military. When asked if the idea of speaking to the general intimidated her, the nun replied, "Why should I be afraid of *him*? I speak to *God* every day."

Perhaps we've heard the words from the letter of John so often that they don't effect a change in us — that if God so loved us, we must also love one another (v. 11). Maybe we need to learn *how* to love.

There was once a lonely girl who longed desperately for love. One day while she was walking in the woods she found two starving song birds. She took them home and put them in a small gilded cage. She nurtured them, and the birds grew strong. Every morning they greeted her with a marvelous song. The girl loved the birds very much and wanted their singing to last forever.

One day the girl inadvertently left the cage door open. The

larger and stronger of the two birds flew out. The girl watched anxiously as he circled high above her. She was so frightened that he would fly away and she would never see him again that as he flew close, she grasped at him wildly, caught him, and clutched him tightly. Suddenly she felt the bird go limp. Opening her hand, she stared in horror to see that the bird was dead. Her desperate clutching had killed him.

Noticing the other bird teetering on the edge of the cage, she could sense his great need for freedom, his need to soar into the clear blue sky. She lifted him from the cage and tossed him gently into the air. The bird circled once, twice, three times.

The girl watched delightedly at the bird's obvious joy. Her heart was no longer concerned with her loss. She wanted the bird to be happy. Suddenly the bird flew closer and landed softly on her shoulder. It sang the sweetest melody she had ever heard.

The fastest way to lose love is to hold onto it too tightly; the best way to keep it is to give it — *wings!*

An anonymous pundit reminds us that, after loving a while, you learn the subtle differences between holding a hand and chaining a soul; and you learn that love doesn't mean leaning, and company doesn't mean security; and you begin to learn that kisses aren't contracts, and presents aren't promises, and you begin to accept your defeats with your head up and your eyes open, with the grace of an adult, not the grief of a child.

You learn that there are only a few shades of connotation separating devotion from obsession. You decorate your own soul instead of waiting for someone to bring you flowers. And you learn that you really can endure, that you really are strong, and you really do have worth. And you learn and learn. With every good-bye you learn.

1 Jn 4:19-5:4; Lk 4:14-22

Watch Jesus Closely

In today's gospel we look at another revelation of God through Jesus. St. Luke tells us that at this point Jesus withdrew from Judea into Galilee. Luke gives the *fundamental motive* for Jesus' move into Galilee as being the divine plan and inspiration of the Holy Spirit. St. John's gospel adds that in Judea, Jesus' disciples were baptizing more people than was John the Baptist, and the hostility of the Pharisees was increasing now. The Pharisees would be more watchful of Jesus because of his growing influence with the people.

Throughout the Jewish world, the ruler of a synagogue could invite any willing adult Jewish man to read the scripture of the day and deliver a homily on it. Today Jesus accepted this invitation. As was customary, he stood up (v. 16) to read and sat down (v. 20) to deliver the homily. Visitors from other Jewish communities were often called upon; the Apostles later made frequent use of this opportunity to preach the gospel. The synagogues were minor places of religious assembly among the Jews; they were used also as schools, libraries, and halls of judgment, and for other less solemn religious functions than those held in the Temple. The main space was for men, there was a gallery reserved for women, and the worshipers all faced toward Jerusalem and the Holy of Holies.

The reading of a definite book was determined by the season, but the passage to be read and commented upon was left to the choice of the preacher. He was permitted to combine texts from the same book. On this occasion in Nazareth, Jesus took the opportunity to collate several passages from Isaiah (61:1f. and 58:6). To promise to bring glad tidings to the poor and to let the oppressed go free were wonderful words that foretold the Messiah. So was the promise to proclaim release to the captives, which referred to the custom of proclaiming the fiftieth year as the "jubilee," when all debts were to be remitted and captives and slaves set free.

The announcement of this village carpenter that these Sacred Scriptures were fulfilled in him was genuinely dramatic, and the whole community wondered at this proclaimed presence of God's power in their midst. The verses after today's gospel inform us that, as Jesus continued, the people in the synagogue remembered his relatives and his previous life among them; so they refused to believe in him.

In truth, Jesus was as fully human as any of us. Even though he was miraculously conceived, like any other child he came to birth after nine months within his mother's womb. He spent long silent years at Nazareth as infant, boy, and young man. In the home in which he grew up, Joseph and Mary's way of looking and exchanging glances of special love, their way of entertaining friends and of discussing their work and the child's education, all showed an ideal married couple.

As he grew, God's Son knew how it felt to be cold, or tired, or sore with pain, because he, too, had a body. He spent long hours, for years at a time, doing the routine and unspectacular work of a carpenter, walked long days over dusty roads with tired feet, curled his shoulders against the night air or a chill rain, was sometimes without sleep, was thirsty and hot and exhausted. He must have known what it's like to wake up stiff on a dull, gray morning, must at times have been anxious and annoyed and irritated. He knew what it means to feel the cool touch of his mother's hand on fevered flesh, to taste the salt of sweat and tears, to hear music and birdsong — and the vilest of insults. On the way of the cross he stumbled and fell, bruised and mangled and torn. He cried out at last, as have most of us at one time or another, to be spared any more suffering.

Now, filled with wrath, the authorities in Nazareth ran him

out of town, intending to kill him by throwing him from one of the hills on which Nazareth was built into the valley of Esdraelon below. But he passed through the mob, because his time for dying had not yet come. The Nazareans were so hard-hearted, however, that he could no longer work miracles among them and had to move his mother and his center of operations to Capernaum.

Today's first reading, from the First Letter of St. John, enhances the importance of the commandment of loving others. This portion of the letter tells us that we can't love God unless we have faith and live the commandments. The commandments are about our relationship with self, with God, and with others. The proof of love for God consists in keeping His commandments, the greatest of which, after love for God, is love of the brothers and sisters — that is, those begotten of God.

The divine word shifts from love to faith when John mentions the means by which we overcome all opposition. Faith in this context doesn't indicate a long series of doctrines, only the basic truth of Jesus' incarnation. If we believe that Jesus took on our flesh, then we will love others and seek to do so heroically. Practical faith of this kind confers a power that conquers the world of evil, just as Jesus overcame it.

The Pharisees watched Jesus closely to get something on him. We, under the guidance of the Holy Spirit, ought to watch Jesus closely for another reason: to discover the message of God in our life. Such glimpses of God will better enable us to acknowledge Jesus as our Redeemer and come to the glory of his kingdom, as we prayed to do in today's opening prayer.

Friday after Epiphany or January 11

1 Jn 5:5-13; Lk 5:12-16

We Can Be World Conquerors

History has shown many self-styled conquerors of the world from Tiglath-Pilesar through Alexander the Great and Julius Caesar and Napoleon to Hitler. Today's beautiful passage from the First Letter of St. John asserts that the true conquerors of the world are Jesus and all those who believe in him. That belief has the firm foundation of the testimony of the Holy Spirit and Jesus' own blood. It's Jesus who gives us the life of God.

To share in that life, we must have faith in and obedience to Jesus — just as the leper in today's gospel did. Because of fear of contagion, repugnance inspired by leprosy, and the legal uncleanness which tainted the victim, there were laws that banished lepers from contact with other people. Those who were thought to be lepers were compelled to don funereal garb and denounce themselves to passers-by, shouting "unclean!" The leprosy of that time needn't be identified with the disease known as leprosy today. Several diseases of the skin were called by this name in scripture. Today's cure was, nevertheless, miraculous.

The leper approached Jesus with a combination of love, trust, and respect. He bowed to the ground. He showed his faith in his beautiful prayer that if the Lord wanted to cure him, he would. Jesus' compassionate response disregarded the ceremonial taboo against touching a leper and so, becoming unclean himself, Jesus stretched out his hand to touch him — to touch a leper! The gospel's simple declarative sentence reveals the infinite depths of divine compassion: "I do will it. Be cured."

Some physical contact was the usual procedure in most of the miraculous cures worked by Our Lord. He did that to show his sympathy for the afflicted person, and — more particularly — to conceal the entirely miraculous nature of these cures by using customary ceremonies. Most of Jesus' miracles weren't done primarily to prove to his immediate audience that he was the Messiah, but rather out of sympathy for the afflicted.

This whole episode represented a mission to outcasts: those distended with pain, those the law can't cleanse, people at the margins of society. Jesus told the cured leper both to go to the priest and to tell no one. The requirement that the cured leper present himself to the priest was, besides testifying to the genuineness of the cure, an exercise in obedience.

Obedience is a virtue which makes us very pleasing to God; it's accompanied by many graces and fruits. The gospel gives us many other examples of persons who knew how to obey: the servants at the wedding reception at Cana, the shepherds in Bethlehem, the Magi at his birth. Jesus, by his obedience, brought about our redemption. His obedience reached its culminating point in Gethsemane, when he completely renounced his own will in order to obey his heavenly Father and accept the burden of the sins of all the world.

Obedience, which always involves subjection and self-giving, isn't a lack of freedom or maturity. On the contrary, what threatens true freedom is disordered sensuality, narrow-mindedness originating in selfishness, and the desire to do as you please. Obedience brings about true formation of character and great peace to the soul — the fruits of sacrificing and giving up one's own will for a higher good.

But that has to be *true* obedience. Every time parents *force* a child or superiors *compel* a subject to do something by using their power or authority, they deny that child or subject a chance to learn self-discipline and self-responsibility. Many parents and superiors confuse listening and talking. In fact, when children or subjects are upset or troubled, most parents and superiors don't listen at all. They moralize and preach, criticize, give advice, and demand subjection.

We express our faith in and obedience to God by living out

our baptismal promises, by participating in the Eucharist (where we offer ourselves along with the bread and wine that will become Jesus), and by prayerful reflection on Sacred Scripture. After all that, we reach out. We help others as Jesus did the leper. After that, we don't want our reputation for doing good to be broadcast. Jesus told the leper to tell no one; he wanted only that the cured man be welcomed back into society. He didn't want people following him for the wrong reasons.

Luke concludes today's passage by telling us that Jesus often retired to deserted places and prayed. As we approach the end of the Christmas-Epiphany cycle, graced with the celebration of the incarnation of God's Son and impressed by the dimensions of his revelation to the world, we hear a call for prayer. Prayer is that internal attitude by which we realize in faith how God's Holy Spirit is abiding within us and within all the people and events of our daily life. Every word and action communicates so much more than what is said or done, because each event becomes a sign, like the tip of an iceberg drawing our attention to what isn't seen.

The First Letter of John insists over and over upon the incarnation. It describes belief in Jesus who came with "water and blood" (v. 6) — namely, in the incarnation and the crucifixion (both later associated with Baptism and the Eucharist) and with the Spirit.

Lord, please touch my sickness: my weakness, my pride, my selfishness. If you will to do so, you can cure me.

Saturday after Epiphany or January 12

1 Jn 5:14-21; Jn 3:22-30

Rejoicing in the Happiness of Others

The very last sentence recorded of St. John the Baptist in the gospel of St. John the Evangelist gives us the best rule of thumb in our communication with Jesus: "He must increase, while I must decrease." That's a good motto for our lives. There's something healthy even in a secular way about forgetfulness of self.

Once we're absorbed in the work of God, however, another problem arises. Good people can become jealous of other people's goodness. The Baptist's disciples, for example, were worried and antagonized to see more and more of their group going over to Jesus.

We, too, have to be on our guard lest, having overcome the worst aspects of the world, we become entrapped by jealousy and theological hairsplitting. Today's reading from the First Letter of John advises us to be on our guard against idols. "Idols" can be even all those holy objects, relics, sacred practices, and religious privileges over which pious people fight one another. And we find in today's gospel one of the loveliest of all responses: joy in the happiness of others! How often happiness and joy don't exist unless we're the ones experiencing them!

Whereas most citizens of the United States can agree on definitions of a human being's first two inalienable rights in the Declaration of Independence — "life" and "liberty" — "happiness," as in "the pursuit of happiness," is another matter. What Thomas Jefferson left vague, generations have vied to spell out. The pursuit of happiness can both animate citizens' daily lives and tie them in knots.

Happiness doesn't have any legal meaning, whereas "life" and "liberty" certainly do. Whereas you can sue for the unjust deprivation of life or liberty, happiness isn't a word on which you can establish a lawsuit. The pursuit of happiness is the defining passion of a country whose signature voice is the blues.

To Jefferson and his contemporaries, happiness demanded (perhaps crazily to us) a good government. When they spoke of the ideal, they used biblical language: to be at peace under your own vine and fig tree with none to make you afraid. What it means to be happy is to want meaning in life. It's a state of well-being and contentment.

Though one person's happiness shouldn't prevent another's, in practice the multiplicity of people with happiness has led to conflict. There's an abiding struggle between those who embrace happiness as the libertarian ethic of complete freedom, pursuing whatever they want as long as it doesn't harm anyone else, and others who say that what's required is a society that rewards virtue, that actively discourages unhealthy activity, in order to allow the most happiness for the most people. Smokers in restaurants and adherents of sexual diversity always leave somebody unhappy. So the pursuit of happiness can mean the pursuit of limits on happiness.

We're constantly being told that we've failed if we feel unhappy; we're taught to believe that if we're not happy all the time we need anti-depressant drugs. The remedy proposed is the pursuit of still more happiness, advertised as being preferably through shopping. There's little cultural conflict in the pursuit of a washer/dryer or a nice set of golf clubs.

It's another Jeffersonian paradox that the pursuit of happiness, an ideal to which any people might aspire, bundles the arrogance, entitlement, and loose morality that so much of the world hates about the United States. The happiness wars, as the culture wars might be called, get more intense when the rest of the world is asked to play too. The rest of the world — aware that United States citizens represent only about six percent of the world's population and use a far greater portion of the world's resources, and that this country gets rid of what's not functional — consider us a "throw-away society."

In some ways it's amazing that the ascetic John the Baptist, perhaps the most austere-appearing prophet in the entire Bible, himself unmarried or at least never associated with a spouse during the gospel narratives, makes use of a marital image to describe his relationship to Jesus: the groom's best man (v. 29). John's decrease to further the Lord's increase makes him thrill with joy because of his loving heart. He's too noble to be jealous. His chief joy in life came not when he was honored, but when he saw God honored. His is one of the finest examples of rejoicing in the happiness of another.

Throughout the First Letter of St. John, the author communicates that we don't protect ourselves from evil or make Jesus increase by fleeing from the world. Such an action would deny the mystery of the incarnation by which the Son of God voluntarily lived in the midst of the world.

The intimate relationship between God and those begotten of Him creates in His children conformity to the divine will, which gives them confident assurance of receiving what they ask for (v. 14f.). The prayer of Christians for their sinning brothers is in conformity with the will of God, who in turn will restore life to sinners (v. 16).

John concludes his letter with the solemn reaffirmation of the great truths he's spoken about. He again places an antithesis between, on the one hand, God, His Son, and those begotten of God through faith, and, on the other hand, the evil one and the world of those enslaved by him. The Son reveals the God of truth in himself and in those who accept him. He conquers the evil one and, by dwelling in his followers and giving them eternal life, preserves them from the sin of the world and from the idols of false teachings that threaten the Christian community. In furtherance of these thoughts, the Church provides us with the coming thirty-four weeks of the ordinary Church year.

Lord, through your incarnation you're in our midst and through your epiphanies your wonder still abides within the Church. Please help us to use the personal pronoun "I" less, and to be concerned more with increasing *you* in the world.